# Disraeli

*John K. Walton*

## London and New York

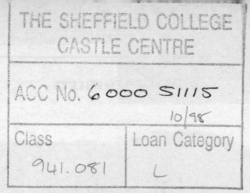

# IN THE SAME SERIES

*General Editors: Eric J. Evans and P.D. King*

First published 1990 by
Routledge
11 New Fetter Lane, London EC4P 4EE

Simultaneously published in the USA and Canada
by Routledge
29 West 35th Street, New York, NY 10001

Reprinted 1992, 1995

Filmset in Great Britain by
Rowland Phototypesetting Ltd,
Bury St Edmunds, Suffolk
and printed in Great Britain by
Clays Ltd, St Ives plc

British Library Cataloguing in Publication Data
Walton, John K.
Disraeli. – (Lancaster pamphlets).
1. Great Britain. Disraeli, Benjamin, 1804–1881
I. Title   II. Series
941.0810924

Library of Congress Cataloguing in Publication Data
Walton, John K.
Disraeli/John K. Walton.
p.    cm. – (Lancaster pamphlets)
Includes bibliographical references.
1. Disraeli, Benjamin, Earl of Beaconsfield, 1804–1881.
2. Great Britain – Politics and government – 1837–1901.
I. Title   II. Series.
DA564.B3W34     1990
941.081'092–dc20
[B]
90-32995

ISBN 0–415–00059–9

# Contents

# Foreword

Lancaster Pamphlets offer concise and up-to-date accounts of major historical topics, primarily for the help of students preparing for Advanced Level examinations, though they should also be of value to those pursuing introductory courses in universities and other institutions of higher education. Without being all-embracing, their aims are to bring some of the central themes or problems confronting students and teachers into sharper focus than the textbook writer can hope to do; to provide the reader with some of the results of recent research which the textbook may not embody; and to stimulate thought about the whole interpretation of the topic under discussion.

# Acknowledgements

My thanks go to David King, for characteristically thorough and probing comments on the original draft of this pamphlet. My special thanks go to Judith Rowbotham, who not only gave me the benefit of her expertise on mid-Victorian colonial policy, but also contrived to suggest improvements and provide insights throughout the text. I hope she will forgive my incorrigible and unrepentant attachment to the practice of beginning sentences with conjunctions. At times I have undoubtedly rejected good advice in other respects as well, and I wish to make it clear that all responsibility for errors remains mine and mine alone.

*JKW*

# 1

# The image and the myth

Benjamin Disraeli is one of those rare politicians whose importance adds up to more than the sum of their deeds. His time in office was short, and he headed only one lasting ministry, at the very end of his career, but he remains a figure of compelling interest, to many of today's practising politicians as well as to historians. The nature and extent of his influence on the long-term development and sustained success of the Conservative Party are matters for highly-charged debate, and the mystique he cultivated was so powerful that mention of his name can still evoke enthusiastic partisan responses, while Conservative leaders continue to squabble over the inheritance of his mantle.

The issues of debate which swirl around Disraeli's legacy are enduring in their significance. At three points, most obviously, he has a high profile in the political history of Victorian Britain. In the first place, his vituperative rhetoric was displayed to savagely damaging effect in the debates of 1845–6, on Catholics and the Corn Laws, which culminated in the defeat of Peel's government and the effective destruction of the new flexible Conservative Party which Peel had been constructing during the 1830s and 1840s. This spectacular rift left the Conservatives, shorn of their Peelite leadership and a significant proportion of their rank and file, to wander the wilderness of opposition and occasional minority government for a generation as die-hard defenders of the Church of England and the landed interest. The importance of Disraeli's part in this is open to

1

question. Was his oratorical contribution an essential, causal element in the course of events, or did his interventions merely affect the language, style and tone of a rift which was bound to occur in some form, at some time in any case? Whatever the conclusion, Disraeli's place at the vortex of one of the great controversies of modern British political history is secure.

Disraeli again held centre stage at the passing of the Second Reform Act in 1867. With a characteristic combination of sheer effrontery and consummate parliamentary skill, he piloted through the Commons a more thoroughgoing measure of franchise extension than the most radical of his opponents had envisaged, enabling his party to mould the details of Reform to its own advantage, but provoking widespread worry among the propertied classes about the potential power of the new working-class electorates of the towns. Within a few years of Reform, the Conservatives were able to reassert themselves as a party of government: although how far this was due to the Second Reform Act, and how far it was made possible by the death of Palmerston in 1865, the rise of Gladstone, and the consequent vacation of the political middle ground by the Liberals, is again open to question. Whatever line of argument we prefer, this was a critical period in party history, with important implications for future legislative programmes and political stability, and Disraeli indisputably played a central part in the Conservative revival of these years.

In this respect, 1867 is part of a longer process, and the fruits of Reform were not gathered in until 1874, when Disraeli won his only election with a substantial working majority. The Conservative ministry of 1874–80 has been, and continues to be, a fecund source of controversy. Some would see it as expressing Disraeli's commitment to social reform, making major concessions to working-class needs and binding sections of the new urban electorate to the Conservative Party, helping to extend Conservatism from its rural strongholds and to rebuild it as a truly national organism. It can also be argued that these years marked a crucial stage in the development of the idea of empire, generating values and rhetorical conventions which were to serve the Conservatives well in future campaigns. But neither of these propositions commands general assent, and arguments which emphasize the building of bridges towards the working class may be thought to sit uneasily alongside the widespread notion that the future of Conservatism lay with the creation of an alliance of the propertied classes, and through the detachment of the commercial and industrial middle classes from an increasingly threatening Gladstonian Liberalism.

Disraeli's activities did not always present such a high profile, but any assessment of the man and his influence must also take account of the formative years of political apprenticeship, before the events of 1845–6 enabled him to thrust himself into the limelight, and of the years of almost unrelieved opposition between 1846 and 1866. He was in his early forties when fame and the front benches claimed him, and hitherto his career had been chequered and, at times, disreputable. He had dabbled in journalism and mining speculation, postured on the fringes of high society, and pursued a parliamentary career under various auspices. Above all, he had written novels, beginning with a high society novel called *Vivian Grey* in 1826. But the works which have given him a lasting literary reputation, the 'Young England' trilogy of *Coningsby*, *Sybil and Tancred*, were products of the mid-1840s, and until these suddenly efflorescent years his career could be summed up in Lord Randolph Churchill's words as 'Failure, failure, failure'. Churchill saw the years of Peel's downfall, and of Disraeli's rise to the leadership of the Conservative rump in the Commons, as a time of 'partial success', but it was followed by another long phase of 'renewed failure' before the eventual achievement of 'ultimate and complete victory' (Jerman 1960: ix). Even so, the earlier years give us insights into Disraeli's ideas, preoccupations and emotions which should not be neglected, and the journalism and literary ventures, though largely stimulated by a pressing need to generate income, provide particularly valuable windows into the thought-processes of an emergent politician.

The years of 'renewed failure' are also important. After the fall of Peel's government, Disraeli's rapid recognition as leader of the Conservatives in the Commons was achieved in circumstances which reduced its value: he owed his eminence to the lack of alternative front-bench talent in a party which had lost almost all its leadership. And the overall leadership remained firmly in the hands of Lord Stanley, who in 1851 became the fourteenth Earl of Derby. The Conservative remnant, though never clearly defined at its fringes, was always the most numerous group in the faction-ridden parliaments of the post-1846 generation, but to stand a chance of holding office for any length of time, a working collaboration with another group was inescapable. Much of the political activity of these years therefore revolved around attempts to forge a Commons majority by attracting former supporters of Peel (who died after a fall

3

from his horse in 1850), or aristocratic advocates of moderate Reform from the Whig persuasion, into a Conservative cabinet. Hopes of such a development were regularly canvassed, without ever coming to anything, and when a Conservative-dominated coalition was not in prospect, Disraeli's energies were devoted to obstructing and dividing the government in power, scoring party points on every possible issue, and even allying with the radical reformers, who were Conservatism's natural enemies on most issues, when there seemed to be some scope for embarrassing or threatening the current incumbents. It was often alleged that Disraeli himself, for various reasons, was the major obstacle to the building of bridges between Conservatives and Whigs or Peelites: some regarded him as an opportunist, others as less than a gentleman, and the internecine conflicts of 1845–6 had left their legacy of distrust and even hatred. In fact, the conditions of these years almost imposed flexibility and opportunism on him. Whether this means that he was really lacking in principle, and involved in politics only for power, fame and glory, is another question, and one to which we shall return.

Many contemporaries were ready to impute ignoble and unprincipled motives to Disraeli, but his eventual success ensured that the image he bequeathed to posterity was very different. Frank O'Gorman crisply expresses the way in which a Disraelian myth has been created and sustained by 'generations of party propaganda, rhetorical exaggeration, literary romance and sheer political nostalgia'. He quotes Arthur Bryant, the quintessence of popular Tory historiography: 'It was left to Disraeli to recreate Conservatism and to lead the crusade of an ancient national party to restore the rights and liberties of the people' (O'Gorman 1986: 30). Above all, Disraeli became identified with the idea of the Conservative Party as the 'national party', providing distinterested and responsible leadership which could rise above class loyalties and represent the British (or, more plausibly, the English) people as a whole. It was in this context that the phrase 'One Nation' became a familiar formula, which was used especially to signpost a Conservative concern with 'social reform'. Such reform was always ameliorative rather than redistributive, of course: it involved protecting groups within the working class from the worst of the abuses which arose from the unfettered operation of a *laissez-faire* economy, but it stopped well short of taxing the rich to improve the conditions of the poor. Even so, quite a respectable pedigree of Conservative support for such measures as Factory Acts, and opposition to the New Poor Law, could be traced back to the 1830s, and here Disraeli's flirtations with various kinds of radicalism in the early years of his parliamentary career could be turned to account.

Two other themes, apart from this concern to 'elevate the condition of the People', became (mainly retrospectively) attributed above all to 'Disraelian Conservatism'. As stated by Charles Bellairs in a Conservative Political Centre propaganda tract, they were 'To maintain our Institutions', and 'To uphold the Empire' (1977: 17). The protection of the established constitution in church and state, with due reverence for the monarchy and respect for aristocratic government in general and the House of Lords in particular, is thus part of the perceived Disraelian legacy, although here Disraeli merely clothed in attractive phrases, most famously in a much-quoted speech of 1872, a Conservative theme which went back to Burke and Bolingbroke in the eighteenth century. Similarly, the idea that Britain had a special imperial mission, to govern and civilize distant races and to spread British settlement and influences to the remotest parts of the globe, was neither peculiar to Disraeli nor originated by him, but it has nevertheless become part of the aura he bequeathed to posterity.

Disraeli was not the only Conservative leader to become a cult figure after his death. Indeed, it could be argued that Conservatism has historically needed such heroes, as part of its concern to emphasize the importance of long-term continuities and the sublime antiquity of the constitution. A mythic interpretation of party history requires a heritage of noble warriors to sustain it. Thus Pitt the Younger, the 'pilot that weathered the storm' of the French wars, was commemorated for many years after his death by Tory dining clubs. Sir Winston Churchill is a much more obvious recent example. Even Sir Robert Peel, not the most obviously charismatic of leaders, was remembered by a spate of statue-building, by a penny subscription fund from 400,000 working men, and by extensive issues of medals and pottery. But this sustained show of gratitude was to Peel as statesman rather than party leader, and it was inspired particularly by the Repeal of the Corn Laws: the very measure which had alienated the bulk of the Conservative Party. And Professor Read concludes that, 'Thanks to a tuneful song, it does seem that John Peel, the huntsman, is now better remembered than Robert Peel, the statesman' (1987: 312). In terms of myth creation, and of lasting identification of policies and attitudes with personality,

5

Disraeli surely stands alone, with only Churchill as a potential long-term rival.

Why did Disraeli, after so long in the wilderness, become a lasting embodiment of a powerful brand of popular Conservatism? Some clues may be obtained from the obituaries which appeared when his death in 1881 produced a remarkable display of national mourning for a politician whose government had been roundly defeated at the polls in the previous year. He was presented as dignified, noble, unselfish in his last hours, and the adjectives which were applied to his career and political personality included 'adventurous', 'imaginative', and above all 'brilliant' (Jerman 1960: 18–20). Disraeli had captured the popular imagination: he had brought romance to politics. He was, after all, an exotic figure: a baptized Christian from a Jewish family, and from a comfortably-off literary background which was still a world away from the aristocratic families who provided most of the general staff of high politics. The social gaffes in Disraeli's first high society novel made this all too clear. His Jewishness, of which he was always highly conscious, made him the regular butt of anti-Semitism in his own party. Indeed, his immediate successor as leader, the third Marquis of Salisbury, referred to him in 1868 as 'a Jew adventurer' (quoted by Steele 1989: 189). *Punch* regularly caricatured him as a shady, wheedling Shylock figure. But, ultimately, his dark and distinctive looks were assimilated into a widely attractive image which encompassed the wit, the ladies' man, the dandy and the virtuoso of debate. Even the cartoonists began to emphasize the romantic rather than the disreputable side of his exotic demeanour. His position as (eventually) a bestselling novelist, unique among prime ministers, helped him to build his own image and cultivate his own air of mystery. The very fact of being a published and much-discussed author also conferred a desirable air of authority, although the really magisterial tone that came from Gladstone's works on theology and other topics of high seriousness remained beyond his rival's reach. But Disraeli went in for inspiration rather than *gravitas*, and as part of this process his origins were often presented as more obscure than they really were, to point up the 'true-life romance' aspects of his rise to power and fame. From the later 1860s, too, his sustained gladiatorial combat with Gladstone helped him to build up a distinctive identity which stood out all the more sharply through the contrast with his rival. The high regard in which Queen Victoria came to hold him, overcoming the utter distrust which she displayed in the early years of his front-bench career, also played its part in the creation of the Disraelian myth: it was she who propagated the romantic notion that the primrose was his favourite flower. In the end, Disraeli contrived to combine the best of all worlds by pulling together a reputation for statesmanship with dash, glamour and literary renown.

It took a long time for Disraeli to turn his liabilities into assets in this way, and to cast off, or remake in acceptable guise, his earlier incarnations as Regency dandy, unprincipled orator and place-seeker on the make, and dissembling political opportunist. Full acceptance did not come until the last few years of his life, when he sat in the Lords as Earl of Beaconsfield, and even Salisbury mellowed towards him. But Gladstone, and the cohorts of high-principled nonconformist Liberalism who took their cue from him in the 1870s, never softened towards him. Even as Disraeli laid claim to the status of European statesman, with his prominent role at the Congress of Berlin in 1878, Gladstone was harrying him as a cynically immoral endorser of Turkish atrocities against Bulgarian Christians. Thus, the controversies about Disraeli's political motives and morality, about the relationship between principle and opportunism in his career, continued to rage at the end of his life. Indeed, they have pursued him beyond the grave.

It thus becomes important to assess Disraeli's motivation, and to evaluate his policies. How much substance is there behind the Disraelian ideal? And how much credence should we give to those who argue that he was interested in presentation rather than principles, and that his overriding concern was with the pursuit, and retention, of place, prestige, patronage and power? Should we regard him as a convinced Conservative standard- and tradition-bearer: and if so, of what sort? Or should we see him as an opportunist who, having hitched his waggon irrevocably to the wrong party at the beginning of his career, was committed to making the best of a bad job and making what he could, at a personal level, out of a difficult situation? It was not just Disraeli's enemies who had doubts about his sincerity and commitment. His friend and close political associate Edward Stanley, the future fifteenth Earl of Derby, frequently expressed reservations in his diary. In July 1850, for example, he commented, 'there is certainly a very prevalent impression that Disraeli has no well-defined opinions of his own; but is content to adopt, and defend, any which may be popular with the Conservative party at the time' (quoted by Vincent 1978: 29). This leads to a further issue which will have to be considered: how far was

Disraeli the architect of his own policies, and how far was he merely the tool of his party or the passive instrument of external events?

To pursue these questions we need to examine what Disraeli actually did, under what auspices, and in what context. Thus we shall address the key themes of the Disraelian legend: the constitution, the Church of England, the empire and social reform. But there is a further central theme which has not passed on into the legend, because it was already losing its central contemporary relevance in the late nineteenth century. It is important, however, because it provided the ladder up which Disraeli began his rise to fame and high office. How important was Disraeli as a defender of the landed interest, and of the predominance of the aristocratic element in the British constitution?

# 2
# Disraeli and the landed interest

On Boxing Day 1848, in a letter to Lord Stanley about the future leadership of the Conservative Party in the Commons, Disraeli wrote:

> The office of leader of the Conservative party in the H. of C. at the present day, is to uphold the aristocratic settlement of this country. That is the only question at stake, however manifold may be the forms which it assumes in public discussion, and however various the knowledge and the labor which it requires.
>
> (quoted by Monypenny and Buckle 1910–20: III, 125)

Lord Blake, in his classic biography, has made much of this statement:

> This assertion is the key to Disraeli's policy for the rest of his life. It represented his profoundest conviction and, through all the labyrinthine twists and turns of his bewildering policy, it remained to the end his guiding purpose . . . his life cannot be understood unless [his belief in aristocracy] is given full weight.
>
> (Blake 1969: 278, 763)

For Blake, what Disraeli sought to defend was not the oligarchic rule of the great Whig landed families, who had been the victims of his angry satire from the very beginning of his political career. Instead, he identified with the rural hierarchy of county society, a great chain

9

of power, status and responsibility which stretched down from the titled aristocracy, through the greater gentry and the squires, to the tenant farmers and the labourers. He wanted to preserve a social order in which the wealth and power of the rulers was justified by tradition, inheritance, education and a shared consensus that property-owners had duties towards their social inferiors and dependants – duties such as protection, patronage and the administration of justice – as well as rights over them. This, we are told, is the central sustaining theme of Disraeli's career. Social reform and the fostering of church, queen, empire and the version of patriotism that went with them might in some senses be ends in themselves, but they were always entangled with, and ultimately subordinate to, the defence of the landed interest and its way of life.

This interpretation commands wide support. Michael Bentley, revealingly, takes these preoccupations almost as a matter of course: when Disraeli's government was beset on all sides, at the close of his career in 1879, 'The Premier turned to the Land for his explanation of political behaviour as naturally as Gladstone had turned to Drink' (Bentley 1984: 229). Ghosh has pointed out that even Disraeli's much-vaunted interest in sanitary reform seems to have found its first expression in a speech in 1864 which exhorted Buckinghamshire landowners to invest more money in improved dwellings for their labourers (Ghosh 1987: 61). The only contemporary or subsequent sceptics about the rooted and predominant nature of Disraeli's concern for the landed interest are those who regard him as a mere adventurer, devoid of true principles of *any* kind.

The only surprise, perhaps, is that it should be necessary to re-emphasize this theme. The need arises more because the Disraelian myth has elevated issues of more obvious twentieth-century relevance on the agenda, rather than because historians of Conservatism and the Conservative Party have misled their readers. Before 1867, says Robert Stewart, 'the party was representative of the land', and land was 'not simply a form of capital; it was the basis of social stability, the natural environment of traditional values' (1978: 368). More recently, Bruce Coleman has placed 'the maintenance of the aristocratic constitution and . . . the interests of landownership' at the core of his analysis of Toryism at mid-century (1988: 99). In this kind of setting, it is difficult to see how Disraeli could have advanced his career in the Conservative Party without a wholehearted espousal of these central preoccupations.

On the face of it, Disraeli can be made to seem an odd, even outrageous, spokesman for the landed interest, and especially for the backwoods gentry of the shires. The dominant self-image of the country squire was bluff, foursquare, plain-speaking, red-faced, corpulent and addicted to fresh air and blood sports: close to the John Bull figure of the *Punch* cartoons, though higher in the social order. The dark, exotic, dandyfied figure of Disraeli confounded this stereotype to an almost offensive extent. When Bentley describes his parliamentary performances of the mid-1840s, his exaggerated turn of phrase has the merit of conveying the alien nature of the Disraelian persona: 'He had evolved a style of limp-wristed discourse with a playful eloquence designed to score Peel's cheek with blades of grass' (Bentley 1984: 122).

But Disraeli's attacks carried more substance than this caricature suggests, and he was much more closely in touch with landed sentiments and the aristocratic frame of mind than might be thought. He constructed and propagated the myth that he was descended from the most aristocratic branch of European Jewry, and this enabled him to identify with the aristocratic principle, and to feel a genuine sense of affinity with the English governing classes. His particular brand of literary brilliance and amusing repartee ensured him a welcome in salon society, and he was never out of place in the country houses of the aristocracy. He had enjoyed direct experience of the life and responsibilities of a country gentleman long before he took over the Hughenden estate in his beloved Buckinghamshire in 1848. Since 1828 his father Isaac, a well-known and prosperous literary figure, had been effectively squire of Bradenham, a picturesque village in the Chilterns near High Wycombe, and at Hughenden itself he enjoyed the society of the neighbouring county gentry. The reminiscences which he prepared in the early 1860s reveal his fascinated interest in aristocratic gossip and the history of ancient families, and he even developed a romantic interest in the skills and attributes of his estate workers:

> I find great amusement in talking to the people at work in the woods & grounds at Hughenden. . . . I like very much the society of woodmen. Their conversation is most interesting – quick and constant observation, & perfect knowledge. . . . Their language is picturesque; they live in the air, & Nature whispers to them many of her secrets. . . . To see Lovett, my head-woodman fell a tree is a work of art.
>
> (quoted by Swartz and Swartz 1975: 117–18)

11

Disraeli had much more interest in, and affinity with, landed society and country living than either Peel or Salisbury, and although his own status as squire of Hughenden had to be manufactured with the financial support of Lord George Bentinck and his brothers, sons of the Duke of Portland, it was in no sense absurd or out of character.

The most obvious and controversial expression of Disraeli's assumed role as parliamentary spokesman for the landed interest was his leading part in the struggle against the repeal of the Corn Laws in 1846. It was this episode, coupled with the subsequent – and consequent – fall of Sir Robert Peel's government, that opened the way to Disraeli's eventual, but not inevitable, leadership of a transformed Conservative Party. This might seem a straightforward expression of his identification with the political and economic interests of the gentry and their tenants. In practice, it was altogether more complicated.

The debate over the Corn Laws had symbolic as well as economic importance. The repeal of the duties on imported grain, making English agriculture vulnerable to competition from the farmers of other nations, was a logical extension of the free trade policies which had become orthodox among governments and their advisers, if not among the electorate at large. But it also seemed to threaten the finances, and therefore ultimately the power, of the landed aristocracy and gentry. It appeared to advance the interests and express the growing power of the industrial and commercial middle class, the 'millocracy' and 'moneyocracy', at the expense of the traditional rulers. It was an expression of class conflict, and it was seen in this way at the time, as the campaigns of the Anti-Corn Law League from 1838 onwards built upon an established rhetoric of opposition to landed domination and mounted a sustained attack on the corruption of aristocratic government. Peel's decision to repeal the Corn Laws, which was taken at the end of 1845, was seen by many of his party as a betrayal of his election promises and of the interests of the class and system of government which he was supposed to represent. It was in this highly-charged setting that Disraeli came to the fore.

Perhaps the most important turning point in Disraeli's career came in the debate on the programme for the coming session on 22 January 1846, when repeal dominated the agenda, and his eloquent, witty, angry and highly personal attack on Peel rallied the forces of agricultural protection and gave articulation and hope to the country gentlemen on the Conservative back benches, who had lacked a spokesman to put their distrust and dismay into appropriate words.

It was this intervention that confirmed Disraeli's reputation as a formidable parliamentary orator, drove a wedge between Peel's followers on the front bench and the back-bench squires, and set in motion the chain of events which culminated in the splitting of the Conservative Party and the secession of most of its established, and potential, ministerial talent. Disraeli could not have risen to the party leadership without this upheaval, but the necessary cost was a long period of parliamentary opposition, punctuated only by short spells of minority government. Whether Disraeli foresaw all this at the time is, of course, another matter.

Disraeli's emergence as a leading spokesman for the agricultural interest in 1846 was anomalous. His advocacy of the preservation of an aristocratic constitution had not led him into the company of the agricultural protectionists: he had been more interested in constitutional theory than in economic policy. He had defended the Corn Laws in the Commons in 1838, but he had not taken a sustained interest in them. His intervention in the debate was couched in the form of an attack on Peel, for changing his policy without consulting the electorate or listening to the views of his supporters, rather than as a defence of agricultural protection as such.

Protectionism was not a deeply-rooted central tenet of Tory philosophy, nor was it a matter of principle for its defenders: as Coleman points out, 'Most Tories argued that the Corn Laws were simply an expedient warranted in particular circumstances of economic interest and political prudence and claimed that those circumstances existed' (1988: 119). The situation in 1846 was inflamed by the rhetoric of the Anti-Corn Law League, and it is not surprising to find that when the heat went out of the issue, Disraeli was quick to seek ways of distancing himself and his party from any commitment to restoring the Corn Laws in any form. In 1849 he was said to have remarked, in conversation with Palmerston, 'Search my speeches through, and you will not find one word of Protection in them' (quoted by Stewart 1978: 223). Edward Stanley, who reported this saying, commented that, 'Whether genuine or fictitious, [it] is near the truth. His great displays on the Corn question have been all attacks on opponents, not assertions of a principle' (ibid.: 243 n.58).

So, although Disraeli rose to eminence through the protectionist wing of the divided Conservative Party, he was never really a protectionist. Recognition of this fact may have heightened the distrust with which the back-bench squires continued to regard him. The protectionist press at first displayed mixed feelings about his 22

13

January speech. 'Nothing could be in worse taste' than his invective against Peel, which was motivated by 'private spleen', said the *Standard* (Read 1987: 210–11). And indeed, it was well known that Disraeli's sustained gadfly opposition to Peel, which was an established theme of parliamentary politics by 1846, had begun when the prime minister refused him a place in his new government in 1841. But as it became clear that Disraeli was the ablest mouthpiece of the Tory opposition to Peel, so his speeches began to be more widely, fully and sympathetically reported, and his credibility among the party faithful grew. Even so, there was at first no question of his being formally recognized as a leader of the emergent protectionist party. Lord George Bentinck was the first to take on this mantle. Despite his lack of active parliamentary experience and his painful defects as an orator, and in spite of his refusal to seek political advantage in the usual ways by the arts of compromise and horse-trading, Bentinck's aristocratic lineage and gentlemanly reputation gave him an acceptability which Disraeli could not yet hope to emulate. And he accepted Bentinck's leadership, supported him loyally, and wrote an extravagantly hero-worshipping commemorative biography after his death.

When Bentinck was pushed out of the leadership at the end of 1847, Disraeli was still viewed too generally with too much suspicion to be able to fill his place. Lord Stanley, soon to be the fourteenth Earl of Derby, led the protectionists from the House of Lords, and for a while Disraeli, much to his own annoyance, was asked to form one of a triumvirate of leaders in the Commons. But his companions, the elderly Herries and the lightweight Marquis of Granby, soon faded into the background. During 1849 Disraeli emerged as unchallenged Tory leader in the Commons. As the Duke of Newcastle recognized, 'we must of necessity choose the cleverest man that we possess' (quoted by Stewart 1978: 234).

Disraeli's rise may not have been instant, and plenty of reservations were still being expressed about his personality and attitudes. He continued to depend upon the legitimacy which was conferred by Derby's overlordship of the party as a whole, and his position was never to be secure until the 1874 election had been won. But his ascent from back-bench obscurity in the late 1840s was still remarkably rapid. Once in place as leader in the Commons, moreover, he became, in his own personality, the best guarantor of his continuance in authority. The return of the Peelites was crucial, in the short run, to the Conservatives' prospects of forming a majority

14

government: their votes, numbering as they did perhaps eighty-five or ninety in 1847 and still thirty-five or forty in 1852, held the balance in the House of Commons. They also contained several men of proven ministerial timber, including aspiring younger politicians like Gladstone, Cardwell and Sidney Herbert as well as older hands like Aberdeen and Sir James Graham. If the Conservatives were to lure the Peelites back into the fold, therefore, they could hope once more to become a party of government, but at a high personal cost to Disraeli himself, whose pre-eminence would be challenged by the return of several of his own personal enemies. But there was little hope of regaining the Peelites while Disraeli dominated the Conservative front bench, symbolizing the feuds which had precipitated and confirmed the split in the first place.

The other great obstacle to the reuniting of the party was, of course, protection, and it was ironical that the enduring strength of feeling on this issue among the Tory rank and file should have helped to sustain Disraeli's position, for he was, if left to himself, no protectionist. But this did not mean that he had no concern for the economic interests of landed society. Quite the contrary: although he saw the Corn Laws as beyond resuscitation, he was eager to find other ways of compensating the agricultural interest for the loss of its special fiscal position in 1846. His thought-processes on this issue were well expressed in the budget proposals which he produced during his short and unexpected stint as Chancellor of the Exchequer in 1852.

Disraeli's emergence as chancellor in the Conservative minority government of 1852 was the subject of much adverse comment at the time. He shared the general opinion that high finance was not his strong point, and tried to hold out for a less uncongenial office, but Derby reassured him with the words, 'You know as much as Mr Canning did. They give you the figures' (quoted by Blake 1969: 311). But he seized the opportunity to provide a novel package of financial proposals. The party had formally abandoned its commitment to protection at the 1852 General Election, and Disraeli was free to explore alternative ways of bolstering the finances of the gentry and their tenants. He had been thinking about this issue since 1848, and had aired proposals for six possible alternatives, the most promising of which were rate relief for landowners, the reduction or repeal of the malt tax (which would reduce beer prices and benefit the growers of barley as well as the brewers and the drinking classes), and reduced liability to income tax for tenant farmers (Ghosh 1984:

15

269). But his problem was to present a measure of relief in such a way that it satisfied the landed interest without seeming to favour the land unduly in the eyes of rival interest groups. The actual proposals involved the levying of income tax at a lower rate on earned than unearned income, with special concessions for farmers, whose income was to be assessed for tax purposes on one-third of their rental instead of half. Disraeli also planned to halve the malt tax, which had long been a subject of complaint and campaigning by Tory back-benchers and their constituents. This could be presented as a free trade measure which Whigs and Peelites ought in all consistency to support, and it was accompanied by a commitment to a sharp reduction in the tea duty, by stages, over the next six years. To pay for this, and to achieve the budgetary surplus which financial orthodoxy expected, Disraeli planned to double the tax on houses and to extend it to cover all houses rated at £10 per year.

This was generally agreed to be an ingenious budget, and the speech of over five hours with which Disraeli introduced it was well received. It had been conceived under severe constraints, because the original calculations had been overtaken by pressure for increased military spending in face of a perceived threat from Louis Napoleon's France. The great Whig historian Macaulay was unfair in stigmatizing it as 'nothing but taking money out of the pockets of people in towns and putting it into the pockets of growers of malt' (quoted by Blake 1969: 339). There was much more to it than this. Most recently, Ghosh has described it as generally 'a principled and coherent measure . . . a remarkable attempt to secure the approval of a moderate majority and yet to reconcile this with the prejudices and interests of the landed men who sat behind Disraeli': a necessary way of building a wider Conservative constituency for the future (Ghosh 1984: 281). This interpretation does not command general agreement, and the budget as a whole encountered magisterial opposition from the guardians of financial orthodoxy among the Whigs and Peelites. It was eventually defeated by nineteen votes, and the Conservatives duly returned to the opposition benches. But the episode does clearly illustrate Disraeli's overriding concern for the financial well-being of landed society, even as he tried to broaden his party's appeal and lead it in from the political wilderness of protectionism.

Fifteen years later, the Second Reform Act provides a further illustration of Disraeli's concern to use a necessary measure of reform to sustain the threatened power and flagging fortunes of the landed interest. It was expressly intended to make the electoral world a more congenial place for Conservatives. The extension of the franchise to male householders (and some lodgers) in the boroughs, which brought an enormous increase in the number of working-class voters, was the main focus of heated controversy at the time, but the important thing for Disraeli and his party was to sustain and strengthen the influence of the landed Conservatism of the counties and the small boroughs. Under the provisions of the 1832 act, many householders in boroughs were able to vote in the county constituencies. Most of these votes went to the Conservatives' opponents, reducing their hold in what were generally expected to be their strongholds. The 1867 act removed these urban voters from the counties: a coup which had already been attempted in the previous Conservative Reform Bill in 1859. Not only were Liberal and radical influences in rural seats thus reduced, the relative importance of the counties was also enhanced in the Commons as a whole. Conservative control over the redistribution of seats enabled the English counties to increase their share of the 658 Commons seats from 144 to 169, and a very large number of small boroughs also survived, in which the influence of nearby landowners was often strong, and sometimes overwhelming, even under the wider urban franchise. The Conservatives were careful to make only minor changes to the voting qualification in the counties: the floodgates of democracy were opened only in a small and conspicuous minority of large industrial and commercial boroughs. Coleman effectively sums up how neatly the whole thing was managed:

> The constituencies which the Conservatives most feared gained little [from redistribution]. London, which on a weighting for its electorate might have expected some 60 extra members, received only a handful. . . . The measures of 1867–68 were notable . . . for how little they changed the old pattern of constituencies and the social balance of county politics. The established interests among which the Conservatives were so strongly represented had escaped relatively unscathed.
>
> (Coleman 1988: 136)

Disraeli was a key figure in the formulation of these policies, although it would be difficult to tease out the exact extent of his contribution to a measure whose detailed characteristics owed much to compromise and concession in the cut and thrust of debate. The important point is that the aspects of the Second Reform Act which protected the political influence of the aristocracy and gentry in the county seats were more fundamentally Disraelian in their philosophy than were the self-consciously daring concessions to urban democracy. Perhaps the crucial effect of the whole measure, apart from the boost it gave to party morale, was that it gave an additional lease of life and legitimacy to the aristocratic constitution whose defence gave shape and focus to Disraeli's whole political career.

The defence of the aristocratic constitution was a much more sustained and clear-cut theme in Disraeli's political life than the narrower protection of the finances of the landed interest, although ultimately, of course, the one depended on the other. As a theme, it can be traced back very early in Disraeli's writings. A recurrent motif of his literary output in the 1830s, *before* the more overtly political novels of the famous 'Young England' trilogy, was the need for a politics based on tradition and national unity, rather than on a competitive individualism which divided and threatened the social order.

Disraeli's philosophy of history and politics is most clearly displayed in the *Vindication of the English Constitution*, which was published in 1835. It was written at the behest of Disraeli's new patron, Lord Lyndhurst, who was in some ways a disreputable figure but was, even so, a senior and influential Tory politician. We might be tempted to regard this as a tainted source: Disraeli writing what his mentor and paymaster wanted to read and disseminate. But it chimes in too harmoniously with Disraeli's later attitudes to be easily dismissed in this way, and Blake is confident that 'we can assume that he meant what he said here, whereas in the novels we can never be entirely sure' (1969: 129).

The *Vindication* develops the thesis that the national identity of England is bound up with its ancient orders and institutions: crown, Lords, Commons, church, corporations and magistrates. The historic role of the Tory Party has been to uphold and sustain these institutions in a manner which makes them expressive of, and responsive to, the truest, highest interests of the English people at large. The Whigs, meanwhile, have consistently sought to subvert and undermine these historic pillars of the constitution in their attempts to capture control of the country in the interests of a clique of corrupt aristocrats. Much of the *Vindication* is devoted to an assertive, romantic justification of this view of history, from the thirteenth century onwards, and to comparisons with foreign systems of government, with the aim of demonstrating that the English

18

are uniquely fortunate in the tradition of government they have inherited, and that they tamper with it at their peril. Particular scorn is reserved for the advocates of abstract systems of political theory, deduced from first principles rather than inherited from ancestral wisdom, and within this framework Utilitarians and Benthamites come in for the most outspoken denunciation. They had, indeed, already been satirized in Disraeli's fantasy novel, *Popanilla*, in 1828. For Disraeli, the doctrine, espoused by the Whigs, that people are motivated solely by a narrowly economic self-interest, and that the duty of government is to give free rein to that self-interest while managing its excesses from the centre, would lead to the collapse of the constitution, of national identity and of English civilization. Here are his views on the consequences:

> Without [our great national institutions], the inhabitants of England, instead of being a nation, would present only a mass of individuals governed by a metropolis, whence an arbitrary senate would issue the stern decrees of its harsh and heartless despotism. A class of the subjects, indeed, might still possess the fruitless privilege of electing its representatives in Parliament, but without any machinery to foster public spirit and maintain popular power . . . we should soon see these mock representatives the mere nominees of a Praefect, and the very first to tamper with our privileges and barter away our freedom. In such a state of society . . . no public avenues to wealth and honour would subsist save through the government . . . and from the harsh seat of the provincial governor, to the vile office of the provincial spy, every place would be filled by the ablest and most unprincipled of a corrupted people.
>
> (Disraeli 1835: 181–2)

These were real fears, and Disraeli alludes to recent attacks on the Old Poor Law (which he saw as another hallowed traditional institution, which protected the popular right to subsistence) and the ancient municipal corporations as examples of the Whig threat to the constitution. The England Disraeli wishes to conserve is presented as a true democracy, in which a firmly established social order provides security, but within which the restless and talented can advance themselves by hard work and ability:

> Thus the meanest subject of our King is born to great and important privileges; an Englishman, however humble may be his

19

birth, whether he be doomed to the plough or destined to the loom, is born to the noblest of all inheritances, the equality of civil rights; he is born to freedom, he is born to justice, and he is born to property. There is no station to which he may not aspire; there is no master whom he is obliged to serve; there is no magistrate who dares imprison him against the law; and the soil on which he labours must supply him with an honest and decorous maintenance.

(ibid.: 204–5)

As a portrayal of the actual state of England in the 1830s, this romantic effusion was, of course, bizarre, but we may still take it as expressing Disraeli's aspirations, and perhaps his enduring political creed. Two further points should be made. First, Disraeli's vision of Tory democracy did not involve most people, and certainly not the lower classes, being entitled to *vote*: their needs were supposed to be met by the responsible behaviour of the propertied members of the political nation, who were expected to recognize the duties as well as the rights of property and to rule in the interests of the *nation*, not just of their own class. Second, all the stress was on the *English* nation, and this was no accident. The Scots, and especially the Irish, were outsiders; indeed, one of the current indicators of the essential un-Englishness of the Whig government in 1835 was that it depended for its majority on the alien votes of Scots and Irish MPs. These were to prove enduring themes.

When Disraeli came to write the 'Young England' novels, and especially *Coningsby* (1844) and *Sybil* (1845), the intervening years had wrought changes in his own circumstances, and in those of party and nation. Disraeli himself had entered parliament, as MP for Maidstone, in 1837. He had made a disastrous maiden speech. He had made public his opposition to the centralizing principles of the New Poor Law of 1834, and had expressed an unusual degree of sympathy (though not support) for Chartist petitioners and prisoners. He had made a marriage which was to bring him a new and valuable measure of economic and emotional security, and ultimately of respectability. Most importantly, perhaps, he had fallen out with Sir Robert Peel and the brand of Conservatism that Peel had come to represent, and he had fallen in with a small but vociferous band of back-benchers who shared his ideal vision of an England governed by a responsible, dutiful and socially conscious landed aristocracy.

The *Vindication* of 1835 contains Disraeli's defence of Sir Robert Peel's response to the First Reform Act. *Coningsby*, written in 1843–4, shows no overt hostility to Peel himself, but contains a sustained denunciation of the 'Conservatism' of the Tamworth Manifesto, as 'an attempt to construct a party without principles' (quoted by Blake 1969: 197). Disraeli alleged that Peel's Conservatism was devoted solely to conserving appearances and forms of words, without any commitment to preserving or restoring the realities of the ancient constitution: 'Conservatism discards Prescriptions, shrinks from Principle, disavows Progress; having rejected all respect for Antiquity, it offers no redress for the Present, and makes no preparation for the Future' (ibid.: 197). Disraeli, significantly, preferred the label 'Tory', which he identified with his vision of his party's historic mission, and it was a long time before he came fully to terms with being a 'Conservative'. By that time, indeed, he had consigned the Toryism of Lord Liverpool and his successors to the dustbin of history, and looked to the revival of an older, purer creed, detached from the business-like temporizing with Utilitarianism with which Peel had become identified.

*Sybil* was written a year later, and extends the attack to Peel himself. It introduces the famous concept of the 'Two Nations' – the rich and the poor, who have so little mutual contact and understanding that they might be living on different planets – and pleads for the revival of an idealized feudal concern on the part of the aristocracy (and on that of enlightened mill-owners) to bridge the gulf and ameliorate the condition of the poor. Disraeli attacks the caste-ridden selfishness of the old noble families as well as the unfeeling exploitation of the workers by their middle-class employers. It is not clear, in context, whether he regards the 'Two Nations' as a threat or an actuality, but this outcome is clearly a danger to the fabric of the state, and one which Peel's government is not addressing. These novels extend and develop the political message of the *Vindication*, reflecting the tangibly dangerous social conflicts of the Chartist years and the real efforts of Disraeli to come to terms with the condition of the industrial working class, if only through the perusal of parliamentary 'Blue Books'.

These points deserve emphasis because it is easy to write off Disraeli's 'Young England' phase as either opportunist or emptily mystical and romantic. Young England was a very small, but vociferous, back-bench ginger group, in which Disraeli acted as leading conspirator and guru. His three colleagues, George Smythe,

Lord John Manners and Alexander Baillie-Cochrane, each of whom featured, thinly disguised, in *Coningsby*, had minds of their own, and intermittent support came from several other like-minded back-benchers. They shared a desire to revive an idealized feudalism, perhaps as much for its chivalric trappings of tournaments and armour as for its social implications. As Thackeray's Jeames de la Pluche put it, 'they're always writing about battleaxis and shivvlery, these young chaps' (quoted by Braun 1981: 73). Young England was an admirable vehicle for Disraeli to keep himself in the limelight, and the other members of the loose-knit group sometimes doubted his sincerity. An element of self-mockery sometimes crept into his prose, on this issue as on others. And it is difficult to imagine Disraeli having become involved in this fuzzily romantic aristocratic cabal if Peel had given him the minor ministerial place he craved in 1841. Even so, the aristocratic revivalism of Young England represented a lot of what Disraeli actually believed in, even though he might seek to distance himself from some of its excesses, and we need not assume that his espousal of 'One Nation' Toryism was at all in-sincere, even if we also suspect that his principles might have been vulnerable to the temptations of office.

The Young England phase was short-lived. By the time *Tancred*, the third and least successful of the trilogy, appeared in 1847, the group had effectively broken up. There were to be no more novels until *Lothair* in 1870, and no more formal statements (enigmatic or otherwise) of political philosophy. Disraeli became immersed in the daily infighting of a minority party in a politically fragmented Commons, seeking advantage where he could find it, and concerned more with tactics than with strategy or the articulation of grand designs. It was during this period that the image of Disraeli as creative opportunist, educating his party in the need for change as the necessary basis of survival, emerged. Asa Briggs puts this point of view very clearly:

> The first lesson he taught was that the party could not hold together on the principle of stubborn resistance against the spirit of the age. Change was the order of the day. Conservatives had to accept the necessity for change and to adapt their tactics accord-ingly – attacking, defending, snatching advantages, and chasing opportunities as occasion demanded. Conservatism could survive only if it considered something more than conservation. The historic past was alive, but it was also dead.
>
> (Briggs 1987: 272)

There is truth in this, but it is not the whole truth. After the demise of Peel and of Chartism there was less of a threat to the aristocratic constitution. A revived paternalism made its own debatable but genuine contribution to the new, if fragile and imperfect, social stability of the mid-Victorian years. Palmerston's ministries were as conservative as the Conservatives could wish for, and it was difficult to mount a sustained and sincere opposition to them most of the time. In any case, Disraeli appears to have had a special relationship with Palmerston, the exact nature of which is uncertain, but it worked towards minimizing conflict between them. Interestingly, Endymion, the hero of Disraeli's last completed novel, founds his parliamentary career on becoming secretary and spokesman for Lord Roehampton, who is modelled on Palmerston, and who marries Endymion's sister (Schwarz 1979: 140). However questionable the half-hidden Disraeli/Palmerston axis may have been, however, and however much horse-trading may have gone on to keep the Conservative Party in business during the lean mid-Victorian years, this does not mean that Disraeli had abandoned the political principles he had enunciated between 1835 and 1847. In the changed political climate, and with his new political eminence, there was no need to restate them, and Disraeli's distinctive vision of a Tory 'democracy' ruled by responsible aristocrats was a commonplace by the 1860s. The visting French academic Hippolyte Taine, for example, swallowed it whole. There was neither the time nor the occasion to go over the same ground again, and in any case the enormous success of *Lothair* in 1870 ensured that the classics of the 1840s were reprinted, to reach a new and apparently enthusiastic audience. Disraeli enjoyed the rough-and-tumble of day-to-day political conflict hugely, and he became a superb practitioner, but whatever deals he might make for specific purposes, the defence of the aristocratic constitution remained at the centre of his agenda. We shall see this more clearly if we look at the narrower themes which supported this great arch, and which went on to make a more lasting contribution in the long run to the Disraelian legend.

# 3
# Church and queen

Apart from the aristocracy, the pillars of the constitution with which the Conservatives identified themselves in Disraeli's time were the Church of England and the crown. Of these, Disraeli himself became associated much more strongly with the latter than the former. His relationship with Queen Victoria became an important subsidiary theme in the Disraelian legend, whereas his own deeds and sayings have contributed little or nothing to the enduring image of the Church of England as 'the Conservative party at prayer'. But to draw this contrast too simply would be profoundly misleading. On the one hand, Disraeli's special relationship with the queen was very much a product of his later years. It did not really begin until his first brief spell as prime minister in 1868, and for much of his front-bench career he was viewed with grave suspicion by Victoria and especially by Prince Albert, who had identified himself very clearly as a supporter of Peel and his policies in the 1840s. On the other hand, religious questions were far too important in early- and mid-Victorian politics for Disraeli to stand aside from them. The position of the Church of England was being challenged on several fronts, and the Conservative Party was expected to defend it against assorted initiatives by nonconformists, Roman Catholics and their allies. Disraeli himself had idiosyncratic views on religion in general, but he was a staunch political supporter of the Church of England, and this theme recurs throughout his career. He could not have advanced himself within the Conservative Party without paying due

24

attention to the earnest churchmen within its ranks. Ultimately, Disraeli's career cannot be understood properly without giving full weight to the religious dimension.

Disraeli's parliamentary career would not have been possible at all if he had remained attached to the faith of his ancestors. Followers of the Jewish religion were excluded from parliament until 1858. But in 1817 Disraeli's father had fallen out with the Jewish congregation to which he and his family had been attached, and soon afterwards all of his children were baptized into the Church of England. Disraeli was a regular church-goer throughout his political career, taking the sacrament at Easter, and maintaining friendly relations with the local clergy. This was, of course, the small change of Conservative respectability, and Disraeli never acquired the more ostentatious and intellectual religiosity which was a Gladstonian hallmark, and helped to sustain Gladstone's reputation as an intellectual heavyweight in the eyes both of contemporaries and of historians. Nor did he become a committed partisan in the internecine struggles between the rival tendencies within the Church of England, and this detachment may well have become a source of political strength to him. However, he never underestimated the importance of the Church of England as a pillar of the state and the social order, nor did he underestimate the power of religion more generally to command the hearts and minds of governors and governed. These perceptions always informed his politics.

The Conservative Party saw itself as the traditional custodian of the special relationship between the Church of England and the state. The same applied to the Anglican Church's sister establishments in Ireland and Wales, and even in Scotland, where the theology and organization of the established church were significantly different but the principle of establishment was effectively the same. By the 1830s and 1840s the traditional arrangements were already under threat. The monarch's position as Supreme Governor of the Church of England was not yet being seriously challenged, but several of the church's privileges were at risk. Some had already gone, like the prohibition on Protestant nonconformists and Roman Catholics holding local office and being elected to parliament. Some had become unenforceable in certain areas, such as the collection of tithes and church rates for the upkeep (nominally, at least) of clergy and buildings. The church was struggling to raise additional money to build and maintain churches and schools, in a desperate endeavour to adjust, belatedly, to population growth and redistribution. Above all, it sought special privileges in educational provision and funding. There were real fears that the church would become a minority institution, as it already was in Ireland and Wales, and as the Scottish established church became, very clearly, at the Disruption of 1843. The Religious Census of 1851 appeared to confirm these fears for England itself, although there was considerable scope for rival interpretations of its findings. It provided additional propaganda for nonconformists who campaigned for the disestablishment of the Church of England, and for the Roman Catholics, whose hopes for the reconversion of Protestant England were beginning to revive in earnest as their numbers, influence and self-confidence began to increase impressively in the 1840s.

The Church of England was thus under siege at the beginning of Disraeli's political career, and it remained so throughout. This was a matter of fundamental importance to most Conservatives, who saw church and crown as mutually reinforcing systems of support which gave moral sanction and justification to the social order and the constitution. If one of these supports were to be removed, the whole edifice might come crashing down. The belief that the Church of England had to be protected as a bulwark against revolution, a protector of property, hierarchy and traditional liberties, was central to the Conservative defence of its privileged position. Significantly, the vast majority of churchmen were Conservatives, and, Wesleyan Methodists apart, Protestant nonconformity identified overwhelmingly with Liberals and radicals.

Conservatives also supported the Church of England because they preferred its forms of worship and believed in its doctrines, of course. But during Disraeli's years the church was not only embattled against external forces, it was also riven by internal conflict, as factions struggled to promote different versions of its identity and message. The Church of England's capacious umbrella covered many shades of opinion and preference. At one extreme was the High Church party, which stretched out to include Tractarians and, later, Ritualists whose services and doctrines were often difficult to distinguish from those of Roman Catholicism with the queen substituting for the pope. There were, indeed, occasional conversions to Rome from this group, which further intensified the mistrust and even hatred with which they were regarded by the militant Protestant evangelicals at the opposite end of the church's religious spectrum. But there were many shades of middle ground, and the politics of the Church of England were a

26

minefield for the unwary, as the parties contended for promotions and authority.

Disraeli was stronger on the church in relation to the constitution than on the internal politics of Anglicanism, which were so important to preferment and ministerial patronage. But in his early years in parliament he was much more idiosyncratic in his religious attitudes than he was to become later, and his independent line sometimes brought him into conflict with the robust, almost unthinking Protestant simplicity of the squirearchical back-benchers who represented mainstream Conservative opinion in the shires.

Potentially most embarrassing was the romantic flirtation with an idealized version of the medieval Catholic Church which became apparent in the 'Young England' novels. *Sybil* shows particular sympathy for the monasteries of medieval England as generous landlords and benefactors of the poor (book II, chapter 5), and *Tancred* gives some currency to the Church of Rome's claims to the special allegiance that goes with antiquity and tradition, despite the corruptions and perversions of more recent centuries. But Disraeli did not allow this passing fashion of the 1840s to influence his political behaviour in parliament. Unlike his Young England colleagues, he voted – and spoke, memorably – against Peel's proposal in 1845 to increase the annual government subsidy to the seminary for Roman Catholic priests at Maynooth in Ireland. Maynooth had been established in 1795, and the government grant had been a source of running controversy through most of its history, with the tempo of angry discussion quickening during the 1830s and early 1840s. One evangelical clergyman asserted that the Maynooth grant 'is paying money to undermine the Throne as much as if it had been spent in buying the barrels of gunpowder which were used by Guy Fawkes' (quoted by Kerr 1982: 233). Peel's proposal actually to *increase* the grant brewed up a storm of protest among the staunch Protestants of his own party. The opponents of Maynooth presented over 10,000 petitions against the proposals, with 1,284,296 signatures. (Machin 1977: 170). A majority of Conservatives (149 to 148) voted against Peel on this issue, and the measure was only carried by votes from the Opposition. This was the first really dramatic expression of the Conservative rank and file's distrust of Peel, and it clearly foreshadowed the Corn Law crisis of the next year. It was important to his future career that Disraeli should be seen to be soundly anti-Catholic on this issue and occasion, and his desertion of his Young England colleagues did him no harm. But this was not a display of principled Protestantism. As Blake says, '[Disraeli] was not really concerned with the merits of the case. He wished to have another hit at Peel and this was an opportunity not to be missed. His argument was essentially *ad hominem*' (Blake 1969: 188).

The importance of maintaining an anti-Catholic stance in recognition of the fierce prejudices which prevailed in his party was made even more obvious to Disraeli by the 'Papal Aggression' crisis of 1850–1. The pope's reintroduction of Roman Catholic bishops with territorial titles into Britain, with Cardinal Wiseman (as he soon became) at their head as Archbishop of Westminster, produced a furious national campaign of resistance in which Tory back-bench opinion was again prominent. Disraeli watched and listened, but said little. His colleague Edward Stanley said of him:

> On the No-Popery agitation at this time raging furiously, D's ideas were moderate and wise. He disliked the movement, would do nothing to increase it, but if it must be dealt with, would try to direct it as much as possible away from the English Catholics, against the Pope and his foreign adherents.
>
> (Vincent 1978: 34)

Some time later, Disraeli spoke on Lord John Russell's proposals for restrictive laws against the new hierarchy, and, significantly, adopted similar tactics to those he used in the Maynooth debate of 1845. Here is Stanley again:

> with a rare ingenuity of debate [he] continued to express no opinion whatever as to the remedies necessary for the occasion, criticising and commenting on those of Government. In this act of censure without self-committal he peculiarly excels.
>
> (ibid.: 38)

Blake's verdict on the episode is forthright. He considers that Disraeli's attitude was 'cynical', and that 'he did not take the papal "aggression" at all seriously from the religious point of view'. But it cured him of any remaining desire to express any sympathy for Roman Catholicism in any form. Henceforth, he acted in the knowledge that 'the "old faith" was a political liability of the first order', and his next novel, *Lothair*, was to show the Roman Catholic church in a very unfavourable light (Blake 1969: 300). At times, indeed, as in 1852, 1854 and especially in 1868, we find him stoking the fires of 'No-Popery' when it seemed electorally convenient to do so, and he fell straightforwardly into line with the mainstream attitudes of his party on this issue.

But there was one set of religious issues on which Disraeli was capable of displaying high seriousness and putting principle before popularity in the party. Stanley remarked in 1851 that, politics apart, his favourite conversational theme was 'the philosophical discussion of religious questions: I mean by this the origin of the various beliefs which have governed mankind, their changes in different epochs, and those still to come' (quoted by Vincent 1978: 31). Disraeli was particularly interested in such issues as they applied to the Jews, and here his religious interests became intertwined with his belief, often expressed, that the ultimate and essential influences on the development of human societies were racial. In the 'Young England' novels many references occur to the ancient wisdom and high aristocratic civilization of the Jews, and the enigmatic Jewish mastermind Sidonia is given some of the best and most intriguing lines. In *Tancred*, especially, it becomes clear that Disraeli views Christianity as a kind of extension of Judaism. Blake expresses this neatly:

> It suited him to blur . . . the differences between the Jewish and Christian faiths. He almost seems at times to regard Christ's Jewishness as more important than His divinity. To him the Jew is proto-Christian, and Christianity is completed Judaism.
>
> (Blake 1969: 204)

This is borne out by a comment in Disraeli's reminiscences, written in the early 1860s: 'I look upon the Church as the only Jewish institution remaining' (quoted by Swartz and Swartz 1985: 103).

These were not wise sentiments to propagate in the presence of Tory politicians who hated the Jews at least as much as the Roman Catholics. But when the status of the Jewish religion became an issue in parliament – after the 1847 election in which the Baron Lionel de Rothschild was elected MP for the City of London and could not swear the necessary oath to take his seat 'on the true faith of a Christian' – Disraeli had the courage of his convictions. Not only did he vote in favour of the resulting bill to remove the civil disabilities of Jews, he also spoke, vehemently and at length, on the issue. He did not argue for religious toleration on general principles, but from his beliefs about the intimacy of the relationship between Judaism and Christianity, and he made himself very unpopular indeed with his bigoted back-benchers. This episode certainly delayed his emergence as Conservative leader in the Commons. And he continued to vote consistently on this issue thereafter, which was more than could be said for his stance on Maynooth. These ill-articulated but heartfelt convictions about Jews and Christians were clearly located right at the core of Disraeli's personality and sense of identity.

More generally, throughout his career Disraeli met the expectations of his party as a defender of the special position of the Church of England. He might not be at home with its dogmas and internal disputes, but he supported the church as 'a majestic corporation wealthy, powerful, independent . . . broadly and deeply planted in the land . . . one of the main guarantees of our local government, and therefore one of the prime securities of our common liberties' (quoted by Blake 1969: 282). So, for example, he gave strong and sustained support to the continuation of the church's power to levy rates for the maintenance of its building and services. In 1861, at least, he justified the forcefulness of his rhetoric to the Earl of Derby on grounds of political tactics, to get the church vote out for the Conservatives in some of the agricultural counties, but this need not undermine the sincerity of his general beliefs about the constitutional importance of the church (Machin 1977: 318). And in 1868–9 he defended the Irish Church against Gladstone's proposals for disestablishment and disendowment, although there was some initial suspicion among his senior colleagues about the true extent of his commitment to this difficult cause. But again, there is no real doubt about Disraeli's sincerity on this issue. Disestablishment in Ireland could be, and was, regarded as a potentially dangerous precedent for the rest of the United Kingdom, and disendowment was a threat to the established rights of property. It is, perhaps, an irony that Disraeli, with his constitutional and ultimately secular attachment to the established churches, should have proved to be a stauncher friend to them than Gladstone, who made such a parade of the exact nature of his convictions and of his precise position within the theological spectrum of the Church of England. But the nature of their political parties, and the composition of their support, limited the range of acceptable policies and behaviour that was open to each of them.

When it came to the internal politics of the Church of England itself, Disraeli's touch was seldom assured. As Blake points out, he was simply not very interested in the niceties of religious politics which preoccupied a large proportion of the political classes, and he affected an air of bland detachment from the struggles between

High, Low and Broad Church and the subgroupings within them. The one central theme in Disraeli's policies was distrust of that section of the High Church party which embraced controversial vestments and ceremonial of an apparently crypto-Catholic kind. This was, perhaps, a logical corollary of his willingness to play the 'No-Popery' card as an electoral weapon, and this was another set of issues on which it was always easier to attack opponents than to defend a position of one's own. When Conservative governments under Derby and Disraeli were able to make nominations for promotion to high office in the church, they tended to favour robust, strongly Protestant evangelicals, and even in the 1860s Disraeli was aware of a 'coterie who hate us and think they have a monopoly of Church championship' among the High Churchmen. (Coleman 1988: 124). And one of the key measures of Disraeli's first majority government was the Public Worship Regulation Act of 1874, which was supposed to make it easier for the church authorites to discipline clergymen who strayed too far in a Papist direction in the conduct of their services (Machin 1987: 70–86). It was unwieldy, and it did not stem the long-running controversy about ritualism in the Church of England. Nor was Disraeli particularly enthusiastic about it. But it was broadly in harmony with the long-term anti-Catholic trend in Disraeli's religious policies after 1850, which in turn expressed his perception (which was not always accurate) of the religious preferences of his party.

The original impetus for the Public Worship Regulation Act had come from Queen Victoria, and she was also a significant influence on Disraeli's church patronage. He tended to view the opportunity to nominate church dignitaries as a useful way of promoting the interests of the Conservative Party, and on the eve of the 1868 election he had tried to secure the support of militant Protestants by promoting controversial exponents of anti-Catholicism. But the queen had her own advisers, and her own well-informed views, and during the ministry of 1874–80 she was able to make a considerable difference to the pattern of nominations and promotions. More generally, as Disraeli well knew, the queen was far from being a cipher. He took great care to emphasize his awareness of the value of her accumulated experience and expertise, and this was not just a matter of flattery, although this was one of the weapons which Disraeli used quite shamelessly in his 'management' of his monarch. The queen's power to obstruct was considerable, especially when it came to excluding obnoxious individuals from her cabinets, and her power to initiate was far from negligible, as the Public Worship Regulation Act illustrates.

Disraeli's vision of the constitution involved the preservation and even the enhancement of the power and prestige of the monarch. At times, indeed, his colleagues feared that he was encouraging the queen to make too many demands on her ministers, especially in the conduct of foreign policy during the ministry of 1874–80. More significant for practical purposes, however, was the nature of the relationship he built up with the queen herself.

Disraeli made a poor beginning in this respect. The queen's attachment to Peel and his policies led her to take a very dim view of Disraeli's highly personal – and highly successful – campaign of abuse and intrigue against his party leader in the 1840s. In 1846 she referred to him as 'that detestable Mr D'Israeli' (quoted by Hardie 1963: 32), and in 1851, when Lord Stanley (soon to be Earl of Derby) was attempting to form a government, he had to work hard to convince the queen that Disraeli was suitable for high office. Prince Albert recorded her sentiments: 'she must, however, make Lord Stanley responsible for his conduct, and should she have cause to be displeased with him when in office she would remind Lord Stanley of what now passed' (quoted by Blake 1969: 302). The Prince Consort himself saw Disraeli as politically unprincipled, and as no gentleman, at this time.

It was not until the early 1860s that the queen's suspicions really began to evaporate. In 1861 the Disraelis were invited to stay at Windsor Castle, and Disraeli's sympathies on the death of Prince Albert were very well received, accompanied as they were by an extravagant tribute to his virtues. The obvious mutual affection of the Disraelis themselves made their condolences on the queen's bereavement all the more acceptable. And in 1863 the Disraelis were highly honoured to be singled out, over the heads of aristocrats and courtiers, as special guests at the wedding of the Prince of Wales, although Disraeli would have been less euphoric had he known that the invitation was a matter of political calculation, instigated by Palmerston, rather than a simple expression of friendship. By 1868, however, the queen found Disraeli personally acceptable enough to have no hesitation in summoning him to be the new prime minister on the Earl of Derby's retirement, even though aristocratic alternatives were theoretically available. And the relationship between monarch and minister became friendly and mutually supportive.

The queen had enjoyed the racy, even gossipy style of Disraeli's reports on the business of the House of Commons when he first held ministerial office in 1852, and his active support for the various schemes to commemorate Prince Albert did not go unnoticed. From 1868, and especially from 1874 onwards, he wooed the queen with flattery and wit, solicitude, and promises of loyalty and devotion, offering to 'render the transaction of affairs as easy to your Majesty as possible' while undertaking to have due regard for her own knowledge and experience. He contrived to cut through the formalities of the court and to engage the affection and sympathy of the lonely 'widow of Windsor', whom he referred to only half ironically as 'the Faery'. Disraeli's wife had died in 1872, and the bond formed by the shared experience of bereavement should not be underestimated. For it would be misleadingly simplistic and cynical to assume that Disraeli's cultivation of the queen was purely a means to an end. He enjoyed female company and emotional friendship, and he also knew where to draw the line in attempting to use his personal qualities in 'managing' the queen. Indeed, she seems to have promoted her own views and interests pretty effectively over the years: the mutual esteem between the two was founded upon a sustained willingness to negotiate and give ground on both sides.

The nature of the relationship between Disraeli and the queen is important because it had consequences. It helped to ensure that the queen became more partisan in her outlook than some thought a constitutional monarch ought to be. This was only partly due to the queen's personal preference for Disraeli over Gladstone, although the Liberal leader came across as too cold, distant, doctrinaire and wordy to pass beyond a formal and constrained relationship with his monarch. It was also a response to the differing policies of the leaders and their parties. Disraeli's Conservatives were less busily involved in controversial legislation and principled dispute over foreign policy than Gladstone's Liberals, and they did not propose measures which might threaten royal prerogatives and interests. The Liberals under Gladstone were increasingly suspect from the queen's point of view on the relationship between church and state, the integrity of the United Kingdom, that of the empire, and even – in a few outspoken cases – the role of the monarchy itself. This pushed the queen, effectively but not overtly, into a kind of tacit alliance with Disraeli, and the frame of mind that this engendered made life difficult for Gladstone at various points in the legislative programme of his governments.

What Disraeli yearned for, but was unable to achieve, was the development of a more positive, visible role for the royal family in the life of the nation. His relationship with the queen improved markedly during the period of extended seclusion which followed the untimely death of Prince Albert, but its success was, in a sense, conditional on his not asking too much of her, and not pressing her too hard towards tasks she found uncongenial or threatening. The queen was administratively very conscientious, but she was unwilling to show herself to her subjects on official or ceremonial occasions, and by the mid-1860s her extended periods of isolation at Osborne or Balmoral were beginning to attract adverse comment. Republican sentiments began to make headway, and were at their height in 1871 when Disraeli spoke in the Commons in defence of her wish to depart for Balmoral before the end of the parliamentary session. Gladstone referred to this as a typical piece of 'flunkeyism', complaining that 'Its natural operation will be to increase her bias against visible public duties' (quoted by Hardie 1963: 61). But Gladstone's attempts at forceful persuasion on other occasions were unsuccessful, while Disraeli did succeed in getting the queen to attend the state opening of parliament on several occasions. He was unable to persuade the queen to agree to a more visible and responsible role for the Prince of Wales, but at times he managed to reduce the amount of time she spent at Balmoral. Hardie sums up by suggesting that on balance 'Disraeli's influence was responsible for the Queen making more public appearances than formerly. If ever there was a touch of Gloriana about her homely figure, it was his doing' (ibid.: 215–16). This is perhaps overdoing it. Most of the great ceremonial occasions, and especially the Jubilees, came after Disraeli's time, and the revived popularity of the Queen after 1871 owed more to popular sympathy at the time of the Prince of Wales's serious illness in 1872, and in subsequent bereavements, than to anything Disraeli did. His own contribution, as a leading figure in the party whose aims were unambiguously to preserve the institutions and practices with which the queen identified, was more on a personal than a political level, although it would be artificial to try to separate these strands too starkly. Disraeli was a loyal upholder of the crown as an institution and the monarch as a person, but his positive and distinctive personal contribution towards the upholding and enhancement of monarchical institutions should not be overstated.

There was, however, one particularly spectacular initiative with which Disraeli was closely associated: the queen's installation as Empress of India in 1877. This episode has become part of the popular view of Disraeli as one of the founders of empire, or at least as one of the most influential proponents of a romantic imperial ideal. In fact, the notion of proclaiming the queen as empress had been current since the aftermath of the great uprising against British rule in 1857. It had awaited a suitable occasion and an, at least, acquiescent prime minister, and Gladstone's intransigent opposition had delayed its coming to pass. It would (so it was hoped) legitimate British rule in the eyes of the princes and their peoples, reinforce the British view of how Indian society and government ought to work, and enhance the queen's prestige *vis-à-vis* the existing European emperors, especially the recently elevated German kaiser. Disraeli was in favour of all this, but 1876 was not a convenient time politically to put such a measure through parliament, and the timing of the measure was entirely due to pressure from the queen herself. What Disraeli provided has been described as 'hyperbolic historical fantasy' (Cohn 1984: 184). His speeches stressed the antiquity and diversity of India's heritages and traditions: an emphasis which of course enhanced the prestige and self-esteem of those who ruled over such an ancient civilization and sought to bring a new rationality and enlightenment to it. The other major Disraelian contribution was the viceroy who presided over the elaborate ceremonial by which the absent queen was proclaimed. Lord Lytton, a poet as well as a diplomat, and the son of an old associate, was a Disraelian appointment, and he brought a suitable sense of grandeur, pomp and myth-making to the elevation of the new empress. This was fitting, and important, and it brings us to a more general examination of Disraeli's role in the development of empire, and in the growth of British power and self-confidence in the world more generally. How much shadow – how much rhetoric – was there in his contribution to the growth of a greater Britain, and how much substance? And how substantial, in its effects on attitudes and behaviour in the long term, was the shadow?

# 4
# Nation and empire

Disraeli's enduring reputation as an enthusiastic advocate of imperial expansion, and as one of the moving spirits behind the new imperialism of the late nineteenth and early twentieth centuries, rests mainly on two famous speeches in 1872, and on the policies and rhetoric of his ministry of 1874–80. The imperial aspect of the 1872 speeches, at Manchester on 3 April and at the Crystal Palace on 24 June, has attracted much more attention from historians and propagandists after the event than it did from the media at the time. Disraeli asserted a need, in the changing circumstances of Europe and the wider world, for more attention to be paid to an active foreign policy. Within this framework, he urged the importance of colonies and overseas possessions in making it both necessary and possible for Britain to play a conspicuous and leading role on the stage of world diplomacy. He emphasized the popularity of empire among the working classes, and he urged that the relationship between Britain and the English-speaking colonies should be placed on a firmer and better defined footing. His peroration at Manchester associated 'the people' and 'the Empire' in a windy but effective passage of rhetoric:

it is not merely our fleets and armies, our powerful artillery, our accumulated capital, and our unlimited credit upon which I so depend, as upon that unbroken spirit of her people, which, I believe, was never prouder of the Imperial country to which they belong.

(quoted by Koebner and Schmidt 1964: 108;
and see also Eldridge 1973: 175–6)

But the sections on the empire were not long or very fully articulated, and they were mainly devoted to attacks on the alleged lack of imperial enthusiasm of past and current Liberal governments, who were alleged to have conducted a sustained but stealthy campaign to dismantle the overseas empire and retreat into an ignoble, money-grubbing Little Englandism.

These utterances were, in the context of the early 1870s, Disraeli's attempt to make political capital out of an existing debate on the colonial policies of Gladstone's government. In 1874, however, he was given the opportunity to put his ideas into practice, and by the end of the decade Gladstone and his allies were accusing the Conservative government of pursuing an aggressive and dangerous foreign policy, which aimed at prestige and domination and threatened constitutional liberties. These issues probably played only a limited part in the Liberal election victory of 1880, but the fact that they were now so high on the political agenda is itself significant. We need to assess the nature, novelty and implications of the foreign and imperial policy of the ministry of 1874–80, and weigh the importance of Disraeli's own contribution. First of all, however, we must address the question of how new these ideas were to Disraeli himself. Some have argued that Disraeli adopted what came to be called imperialism suddenly and opportunistically in 1872, and that the speeches of that year ran directly counter to his previously expressed opinions. Others claim to detect a long-running consistency in Disraeli's ideas. As the 'new imperialism' came to be a central theme in Conservative Party values, and as Disraeli's perceived role in propagating it is so important, this controversy is worth pursuing.

Those who accuse Disraeli of mere opportunism lean heavily on two of his vivid phrases to suggest that in earlier years he had no use for the colonies. In 1852 he wrote to his colleague Malmesbury, 'These wretched colonies will all be independent, too, in a few years, and are a millstone round our necks' (quoted by Stembridge 1965: 125). In 1866 he referred to the colonies 'which we do not govern' in British North America as 'deadweights', and asked what the use of them was. This was an irritated reaction to the Canadians' apparent unwillingness to take proper responsibility for their own defence, in the face of internal unrest, border incursions by Fenians from the United States, and the real possibility of an American invasion. This put the burden and expense of defence on the British government. But this evidence does not take us very far. The comments refer only to old-established colonies in British North America, and not even to all of those: as Hyam and Martin point out, 'Disraeli's millstones amounted to little more than Nova Scotia and New Brunswick' (1975: 3). Even in this context, they reflect a desire to redefine relationships rather than to terminate them, and they tell us nothing about Disraeli's attitude to the other colonies with extensive British settlement. Still less do they offer any hint about Disraeli's attitude to India, or to other territories which were administered from London but peopled almost entirely by their indigenous inhabitants. If we trace Disraeli's views on the British empire through his writings and speeches more carefully, we find that the views he expressed in 1872 are consistent with his declared attitudes over many years. The empire had not been a strong or sustained priority for him, admittedly, but he can be acquitted of opportunistically tailoring his speeches to fit the (anyway uncertain) temper of the times.

S. R. Stembridge showed in 1965 that in his first political pamphlet, 'What is he?', in 1833, Disraeli 'feared the loss of "our great Colonial Empire" and expressed hope that its glory might be maintained'. Through the 1830s and 1840s he argued for the maintenance of imperial authority over the colonies, and accused Whigs and Liberals of undermining the empire. He accepted the argument that 'colonies which governed themselves should defend themselves', and that the relationship between mother country and colonies should be reciprocal rather than exploitative in either direction (at least as far as the English-speaking and English-settled colonies were concerned). In a speech of 1863, arguing against giving up the Ionian Islands, he expressed his attitudes very clearly indeed:

I am perfectly aware that there is a school of politicians – I do not believe that they are rising politicians – who are hostile to the very principle of a British empire. But I have yet to learn that Her Majesty's Ministers have adopted the wild opinions which have been prevalent of late. Professors and rhetoricians find a system for every contingency and a principle for every chance; but you are not going, I hope, to leave the destinies of the British empire to prigs and pedants. The statesmen who construct, and the warriors

38

who achieve, are only influenced by the instinct of power, and animated by the love of country. Those are the feelings and those the methods which form empires.

(quoted by Stembridge 1965: 126–31)

The attack on prigs and pedantry was fitting, for Disraeli had little interest in the details of colonial policy and administration: what attracted him, as so often, was the broad sweep of thematic ideas. His main concern, too, was less for the self-governing settler colonies than for India. Much – though not all – of the foreign policy of his 1874–80 ministry can be seen in these terms. But it is clear that Disraeli's utterances in 1872 were perfectly consistent with what he had said in previous years. Indeed, Freda Harcourt has pointed out that in 1866, in a speech at Beaconsfield, Disraeli had announced that, 'England is no longer a mere European power; she is the metropolis of a great maritime empire, extending to the boundaries of the farthest oceans . . . she interferes in Asia, because she is really more an Asiatic power than a European' (Harcourt 1980: 96). This characteristic piece of grandiloquence was in tune with much contemporary newspaper opinion, and it also stressed England's interest in interfering in Australia, Africa and New Zealand, and indeed in Europe when circumstances might require it, and it signposted the kind of forward, flamboyant foreign policy which found expression in the Conservative government's Abyssinian expedition of 1867. This was a distraction from domestic discontents, and a well-publicized military success. It achieved its concrete goal of freeing a handful of British prisoners, and it also put down a marker in international politics to display Disraeli's intentions for the future: for Harcourt shows that this was essentially *his* policy.

So there was nothing aberrant, or really novel, about the 1872 speeches. Eldridge expresses Disraeli's position on the empire very well, and this was a long-term perspective:

> Disraeli was not interested in the self-governing colonies, except in so far as the remaining responsibilities hampered Great Britain's foreign policy . . . [he] was not interested in the government of indigenous populations or expansion in the tropics, except in so far as these problems affected Great Britain's position and prestige as a world power. Disraeli was a master of ideas, not detail, and it was the part the possession of empire could play in assisting Great Britain's role in world affairs that interested him most.

(Eldridge 1973: 180–1)

All this helps us to understand the actions of Disraeli's subsequent government.

In his celebrated Midlothian campaign of impassioned speeches against Disraeli's government, during the winter of 1879–80, Gladstone paid special attention to foreign and colonial policy. In so doing, he set up an enduring image of Disraeli's aims and philosophies: an image of the reckless and war-mongering expansion of empire, coupled with a more general disregard of morality and financial propriety, and even an intention to subvert the constitution by promoting the personal rule of queen and prime minister. Disraeli was presented as hungry for national prestige above all other considerations, and as threatening to by-pass parliament in the autocratic exercise of imperial diplomacy. This indictment can be challenged in its details, and the partisan flavour of its electioneering context should not be forgotten, but its overall thrust deserves to be taken seriously.

Where Gladstone's attack focused on specific events in South Africa and Afghanistan, his indictment carries least weight, although it cannot be discounted altogether. Significantly, the acquisition of Fiji in 1874 was not made part of the attack on 'Beaconsfieldism': as Gladstone said, 'I don't consider the Government is censurable for that act. . . . Nobody could say that that was their spontaneous act' (Gladstone 1971: 48). The Disraeli government inherited a situation in which the annexation of Fiji was almost inescapable, and the colonial secretary, the Earl of Carnarvon, did little more than carry on the policy of his Liberal precursor. Disraeli's direct involvement was minimal, and an important and easily overlooked aspect of his government's colonial policy was expressed by Carnarvon's injunction to the first governor of Fiji, 'I see very strong reasons for avoiding all possible expenditure that is not necessary' (quoted by Swartz 1985: 11).

More generally, Disraeli left the details of colonial administration to Carnarvon, and to his successor from 1878, Sir Michael Hicks Beach. It was they, and more directly the government's representatives on the spot, who presided over the events which did form part of the Gladstonian indictment:

[The Government] have annexed in Africa the Transvaal territory, inhabited by a free European, Christian, republican community . . . we have made war upon the Zulus . . . and we have, by the most wanton invasion of Afghanistan, broken that country into

40

pieces, made it a miserable ruin . . . [and] caused it to be added to
the anarchies of the Eastern world.

(Gladstone 1971: 48–9)

The South African policy was not a Disraelian innovation. It was
inherited from the previous government, and presided over by
Carnarvon. The aim was to bring to fruition a long-standing
colonial office preference for federation, bringing together the four
British territories and two Boer republics in the region. The republics stood out against persuasion, and in April 1877 Carnarvon
brought about the annexation of the Transvaal. Disraeli's part in all
this was limited to telling Carnarvon, 'In all these affairs I must trust
to you. . . . Do what you think wisest' (quoted by Eldridge 1973:
195). The Transvaal resisted annexation, and the British were
brought into direct confrontation with the Zulus. Carnarvon's
successor, Hicks Beach, reaped the whirlwind in 1879, when Sir
Bartle Frere, Carnarvon's nominee as governor, disobeyed the spirit
of instructions from London and brought about a Zulu war which
began with a catastrophic defeat at Isandhlwana. Reinforcements had
to be sent out, and heavy expense incurred, before the war could be
won. Disraeli felt obliged to support his officials in public, while pri-
vately seething. He opined that Frere 'ought to be impeached', and,
using Carnarvon's revealing nickname, expostulated at one point
that, 'Every day brings forward a new blunder of Twitters' (quoted
by Eldridge 1973: 198). The African events were emphatically not
part of a new aggressive policy of militaristic aggrandizement:
rather, they resulted from a series of blunders and miscalculations
involving inadequate responses to external circumstances.

Much the same applied to the Afghanistan problem. The invasion
of Afghanistan at the end of 1878, the imposition of a British mission
in the Afghan capital, and the further punitive expedition which
followed when the envoys were massacred, were not the fruits of a
Disraelian policy of expansion into and beyond the hill tribe areas of
the north-west frontier. They fell within an existing framework of
policy-making expectations. The problem arose in the first place
because the Afghans had entertained a Russian delegation, and there
were fears that the Russians might have long-term designs on India.
But the conflict was precipitated by the aggressive line taken, on his
own initiative, by the viceroy Lord Lytton in India, and by the
perceived political need to avenge the humiliating rebuff with which
the Afghans had initially responded to Lytton's pressure. Here again,

41

Disraeli's appointee was at fault, and supervision from the centre was inadequate, but as in South Africa, Disraeli's concern was rather to extricate himself from a difficult and expensive situation than to urge his bellicose subordinates forward. In each case, Gladstone's criticisms imputed to the government a systematic, co-ordinated plan of campaign which was in practice conspicuous by its absence.

But there is a little more to it than this. First, it could be argued that the flamboyance of Disraeli's rhetoric on foreign policy issues was all too likely to lead his subordinates into extravagant postures and deeds, whether or not he gave them detailed and specific support. He engendered an atmosphere which was sympathetic to such gestures. His notions of national prestige and honour, as well as national interest, were particularly significant here, and they were not new-minted in the 1870s. Second, the South African and Afghan issues were especially sensitive because they were directly connected with themes which were close to Disraeli's heart. South Africa was important because of the need to safeguard the Cape route to India. Carnarvon was twitchily anxious to extend British influence along the coastline, and he worried about the lack of military expenditure in the area, pointing out that 'If I remember rightly 190.000.000£ worth of our trade pass the Cape each year' (quoted by Swartz 1985: 21). There was more to his policy than a narrow concern for parsimony and security, and the same applies, emphatically, to Disraeli. Gladstone might have been wrong to ascribe the Zulu campaign itself to Disraelian aggrandizement, but he did not distort the underlying attitudes which informed the government's policies more generally.

In the case of Afghanistan, two obsessions came together: the protection of India and the fear of Russia. Disraeli did not share the enduring and systematic Russophobia of some fellow Conservatives, but he did come to regard Russian diplomacy with suspicion, and to entertain strongly-held fears about the threat posed by Russian expansionism to India and its access routes. This suspicion of Russian motives helped to form the climate of expectations which made the Afghan episode possible, and although Disraeli was not responsible for what actually happened, it was not out of line with his general, overriding and well-known concerns.

The Russia and India motifs recur elsewhere, coupled with a concern to assert British prestige, honour and activity on the European stage in ways which some of Disraeli's patrician colleagues found unseemly and even incomprehensible. The famous purchase of the Suez Canal shares from the near-bankrupt Khedive of Egypt in 1875 was justified by the need to have a voice in the management of this key waterway, the shortest route to India, which might otherwise have fallen under the control of French interests. Disraeli savoured the drama and magnified the extent of his success, but this was indeed a major coup, and it is significant that Gladstone recognized its popularity, swallowed his principled objections, and left it out of his Midlothian indictment of 'Beaconsfieldism'. It is also significant that the Suez Canal affair coincided with a crisis in the Malay States to which Disraeli paid little heed, and that he showed scant interest in imperial expansion on the Gold Coast or in Fiji. These developments did not threaten or otherwise affect the heartlands of Disraeli's conception of empire. His enthusiasms were selective, and what really brought them into focus was the Eastern Question, which dominated the foreign policies of his ministry and provided most of the fuel for Gladstone's denunciations.

The revival of the question of what to do about the destabilizing effects of the continuing decline of the Turkish empire was seen by Disraeli as a great opportunity to make his mark as a European statesman. After 1876 it was the dominant theme of his ministry. The issues it raised led Gladstone in 1879 to list the principles of foreign policy which he held to have been violated: the preservation of peace and justice (with economy), the avoidance of 'needless engagements', the acknowledgement of 'the Equal Rights of all Nations', 'to maintain the Concert of Europe' rather than taking separate and divisive action, and to encourage the 'freedom' of nations and individuals (Gladstone 1971: 9). Disraeli, on the other hand, put the national interest, conceived in terms of economic well-being, prestige and reputation for power, ahead of these great moral principles, and this conflict over the nature of the moral responsibility of the state in external affairs gave added sharpness to the struggle.

Disraeli inherited the traditional Palmerstonian policy of trying to shore up Turkey with a view to preventing Russia from becoming a Mediterranean power and securing Constantinople. The dominant concern here was to protect the Mediterranean route to India, which the Suez Canal now made much more important, and Disraeli, at least, saw India itself as being vulnerable to an overland attack from a Russia with a firm footing in Constantinople. As part of this policy it was also desirable to detach Russia from Austria and the new imperial Germany. The pursuit of these diplomatic aims was disrupted in 1876 by the well-publicized massacres of Bulgarian Christians by Moslem irregulars at the behest of their Turkish overlords. This brutal crushing of a movement for national self-determination, which also enlisted the sympathies of Christians against Moslems, brought Gladstone out of retirement to conduct his 'Bulgarian atrocities' campaign, which enabled him to seize the moral high ground and marshal the principled forces of militant provincial nonconformity against Disraeli. Disraeli, in turn, was mystified and slow to react, making it all too apparent that he did not care about the humanitarian and religious issues. Nor had he any sympathy for small nations struggling to escape the Turkish yoke: he could see the potential analogies between Bosnia or Bulgaria and Ireland far too clearly for that. He sought only to protect the established interests of British policy, conventionally defined.

As the agitation faded, new problems emerged. The Russians declared war on Turkey in the spring of 1877, and the prospect of unilateral British intervention, ostensibly on Turkey's behalf, became all too real. In early 1878 Disraeli sent a fleet to Constantinople, and dispatched 7,000 Indian troops to Malta. This last move was intended as a practical expression of the ties and mutual responsibilities of empire, but its constitutional legitimacy was debatable, and it was indeed debated at great length in the Commons. The point at issue was that using Indian troops evaded the necessity for parliamentary approval, and could be seen as a dangerous precedent for further autocratic actions in the future. All this formed part of the Gladstonian indictment.

In the end, war was averted, and a negotiated settlement was reached. Disraeli was able to return from the Congress of Berlin in July 1878 with the famous slogan, 'Peace with Honour', and a new Mediterranean acquisition, Cyprus, to provide a further base from which to safeguard the lines of communication with India. This new dependency epitomized many of Gladstone's objections to Disraelian foreign policy: there were no real cultural ties between Britons and Cypriots, and the only possible relationship would be one of subordination and submission, rather than the fraternal ideal which Gladstone espoused. And the obsession with India, which had brought about this further extension of British rule, would inevitably continue to impel Britain into new commitments, expenditures and international immoralities.

The part played by Disraeli's ministry in the unfolding of this phase of the Eastern Question was less innovatory and less organized

44

or premeditated than Gladstone and other opponents alleged. Professor Shannon argues that Disraeli pursued an essentially Palmerstonian policy, recovering for the Conservatives a position which Palmerston had usurped, and which Gladstone's Liberals had now renounced. Disraeli embraced the enthusiastic pursuit of 'national' interests, defined in terms of prestige as well as trade, and the restoration of Britain to 'her rightful place' of respect and consideration among the major European powers. This was part of a 'natural order' which now needed to be reasserted (Shannon, 1976: ch. 6). But what was conspicuously absent was the characteristic Palmerstonian rhetoric of the defence of liberty and the right to national self-determination. This was *realpolitik* without even a window-dressing of diplomatic morality, and it did have authoritarian overtones which were not just a matter of rhetoric, especially when the queen began to assert herself in bellicose style over the Eastern Question. It was not only the Gladstonians who became uneasy about both the style and the substance of Disraeli's foreign policy. He lost both his foreign secretary, Derby, and his colonial secretary, Carnarvon, during a period in early 1878 when war seemed dangerously probable. Derby was compromised by his close association with the Russian ambassador, but he articulated attitudes which were more widely felt:

> To the Premier, the main thing is to please and surprise the public by bold strokes and unexpected moves: he would rather take serious national risks than have his policy called feeble or commonplace: to me, the first object is to keep England out of trouble, so long as it can be done consistently with honor & good faith.
>
> (quoted by Swartz 1985: 47)

He also confided in Salisbury:

> [Disraeli] believes quite thoroughly in 'prestige' *as all foreigners do*, and would think it (quite sincerely) in the interests of the country to spend 200 millions on a war if the result was to make foreign states think more highly of us as a military power. These ideas are intelligible but they are not mine nor yours.
>
> (quoted Blake 1969: 636; emphasis added)

Derby saw foreign affairs as a cultivated pursuit for aristocrats, with the goal being the preservation of international concord, and by his lordly standards Disraeli's approach was distasteful and unEnglish, as the comment about 'foreigners' suggests. Viewed from a more populist perspective, however, it could seem the quintessence of Englishness. Hugh Cunningham has argued that it was 'in the space of a few months in late 1877 and early 1878' that the issues raised by the Eastern Question enabled Disraeli's Conservatives to hijack the language of 'patriotism' from Liberals and democrats and attach it to their own aggressive nationalism. The crowds who broke up peace meetings and demonstrated in support of war against Russia were organized, in many cases, by Ellis Ashmead Bartlett, who was 'suitably enough rewarded when Disraeli found him a pocket borough in the 1880 election' (Cunningham 1989: 75, 77). This outburst of 'jingoism' (named from a famous music-hall song of the time, which became a rallying-call) gave practical, physical expression on the streets to Disraeli's beliefs about the potential for winning over the new working-class electorate to 'national principles', as articulated in his 1872 speeches: 'They are for maintaining the greatness of the kingdom and the empire, and they are proud of being subjects of our Sovereign and members of such an Empire' (quoted by Cunningham 1989: 75). Disraeli himself had been informed by his private secretary, Montagu Corry, that a fierce attachment to 'the interest or honour of England' had gained votes for the Conservatives at the Salford by-election of April 1877, and it was Corry, too, who reported in similar vein to his master on the sentiments of London's music-hall audiences (Swartz 1985: 60–1, 155–6). This apparent sea-change in popular attitudes could be regarded as the most significant domestic dividend from Disraeli's foreign policy, and one with lasting implications.

This is probably so, but some caution is needed. A strong working-class peace movement existed in 1877–8: otherwise there would have been no meetings to attack, and although it was driven underground, its sentiments were not extinguished. Much of the fervour was carefully orchestrated, as was the demonstration of support which greeted Disraeli and Salisbury on their return from the Berlin Congress. Cunningham points out that an alternative music-hall song was just as popular at the time as the 'jingo' song:

> I don't want to fight, I'll be slaughtered if I do!
> I'll change my togs and sell my kit and pop my rifle too!
> I don't like the war, I ain't no Briton true,
> And I'd let the Russians have Constantinople.
> > (quoted by Cunningham 1989: 79;
> > 'pop' here means 'pawn')

Finally, and again in the short run, the 'jingo' agitation appears to have been short-lived (and at times embarrassing to its political masters when they found themselves trying to negotiate with its clamour at their backs), and it made little discernible impact on the 1880 election result, which was so disastrous for the Conservatives.

One further point about Disraeli's 'national' foreign policy deserves emphasis. The nation at issue was, in practice, England rather than Britain, as speech after speech and letter after letter make clear. Disraeli showed no interest in Scotland, although he was elected lord rector of Glasgow University in 1871, and Wales was irrelevant except for the income from his wife's property there. His main concern with Ireland when in office was to avoid stirring up trouble. The brilliant analysis of the Irish problem which he produced in a few sentences in the Commons in 1844 was never followed up.

In foreign and imperial policy as in other fields, Disraeli's contribution was more a matter of style and presentation than of innovation or (emphatically) administration. He had firm ideas about the overall direction of policy, but he left his ministers on a loose rein except at moments of crisis, and the spadework even on great set-piece occasions like the Berlin Congress was done by others. Disraeli refused to speak French, the essential language of diplomacy, at Berlin, and Shannon even suggests that 'Beaconsfield achieved nothing at the Congress except to be the gratified recipient of Bismarck's heavy flattery' (1976: 134). And most of the Eastern Question settlement of 1878 was undone within a few years. The Disraelian legacy of imperialist rhetoric may have made more of a difference in the long run, but the 'scramble for Africa' and other heady events in the late nineteenth century needed no imprimatur of this kind. Koebner and Schmidt long ago put Disraeli's contribution to British imperialism in perspective. He had no coherent theory of empire, but new ideas about the concept came to the fore during the years of his ministry, partly as an angry reaction to some of his activities:

> the legend which linked his name with imperialism had its legitimate foundation. . . . During the years of his administration a concept of Empire developed which gave the word a new ring of power and confident assertion among the public. It stressed the possession and defence of a considerable portion of Asia.
>
> (Koebner and Schmidt 1964: 133–4)

It also involved: 'the notion of an Empire as a compact entity, ready for combat, commanded from one centre, and relying on its collective military force' (ibid.: 133–4). This, of course, was what Gladstone so abominated. It owed something to Disraeli's 'imperial language', which sometimes emphasized and popularized it, but it was the product of the times rather than the invention of an individual, and it owed most of all to the rise of the great continental empires and the need to respond to their power and pretensions (ibid.: 133–4).

The most important influences of Disraelian foreign policy, and of the associated rhetoric, were felt on the domestic scene. It was used quite explicitly by Disraeli – and, for example, Salisbury – as a distraction from domestic ills and controversies, and as a way of avoiding the emergence of class conflict in a form which might threaten property and order. Disraeli told Derby in 1871 that:

> I am not . . . sorry to see the country fairly frightened about foreign affairs, 1st, because it is well that the mind of the nation should be diverted from that morbid spirit of domestic change and criticism, which has ruled us too much for the last forty years.
>
> (Quoted by Swartz 1985: 25–6)

Salisbury was more direct still: he thought that a revival of British involvement in European diplomacy would 'draw classes together and purify our internal conflicts from the material element which is coming to be dominant in them' (ibid.: 29). So foreign policy became an extension of domestic policy. It should therefore be seen alongside the ideas of 'One Nation' and Conservative social reform which are also associated with Disraeli, and have also generated controversy among historians.

# 5
# Social reform

The image of Disraeli as a key figure in the emergence of a Conservative tradition of concern with elevating 'the condition of the People' has been much discussed, especially with reference to the ideas of 'Young England' and the extent to which they bore fruit in the social legislation of the ministry of 1874–80. As with Disraeli's attitudes to the empire, much has been made of the references to public health, sanitary reform and the circumstances of the working class more generally in the famous speeches of 1872. At Manchester he asserted firmly that, 'Pure air, pure water, the inspection of unhealthy habitations, the adulteration of food, these and many kindred matters may be legitimately dealt with by the Legislature' (quoted by Smith 1967: 159). At the Crystal Palace he extended the potential areas for Tory legislation to include factory reform and the relationship between capital and labour. And the beginning of his subsequent ministry was fertile in legislation in these fields. Paul Smith provides a summary of the 'eleven major acts' of 1874–6: 'In 1874 they dealt with licensing and factory hours; in 1875 with the labour laws, artisans' dwellings, public health, friendly societies, and adulteration; in 1876 with education, merchant shipping and the pollution of rivers' (ibid.: 202). But how much of this legislation was window-dressing, and how much of real value? How far was it distinctively Conservative, and how far the product of something that might be more specifically labelled *Disraelian* Conservatism? Do these measures embody the realization of long-held and deeply-felt

'One Nation' ideals on Disraeli's part, or should we see them as pragmatic responses to immediate circumstances and opportunities?

Most recent historians have followed Paul Smith, and indeed Lord Blake himself, in viewing the 'One Nation' interpretation with considerable scepticism. The legislation itself was of varying quality. Some of it was inherited from the previous government, and merely happened to emerge from the administrative pipeline in the mid-1870s. Some was effectively imposed on the government by outside agitation, at least in its timing and the exact form it finally took. As with the empire, specific policies were the work of individual ministers, and emerged piecemeal, rather than expressing a great overarching programme laid down by the prime minister. Most of the measures fell outside the conventional patterns of party conflict, and their connection with 'Young England' was at best rhetorical. And as soon as issues which were recognized as the proper stuff of high politics reappeared on the agenda to polarize the parties when the Eastern Question 'went critical' in 1876, the flow of lower-status 'social' legislation dried up again.

Of the spate of acts passed on broadly 'social' issues during 1874–6, only the revision of the labour laws was straightforwardly successful. As Blake points out, the significantly-named Employers and Workmen Act (which replaced the Master and Servant Act) and the Conspiracy and Protection of Property Act 'satisfactorily settled the position of labour for a generation', until the judges began to reinterpret them systematically in the employers' favour (Blake 1969: 555). Unions were no longer to be vulnerable to prosecutions for conspiracy or to the prohibition of peaceful picketing whenever a dispute occurred. Organized labour obtained all the major concessions it had been seeking. Disraeli was firmly behind this measure: he realized its importance to working men, and supported it in a generally hostile or sceptical cabinet. But this was in no sense a paternalist initiative: it was aimed at redressing the visible unfairness of legislation which restricted employees more than masters, and it was entirely compatible with the strictest principles of *laissez-faire*. Moreover, it is now clear that the Liberals in 1871 had intended to reach much the same position, and had been frustrated by the insufficiently precise language used by their parliamentary draftsmen, which had enabled judges and magistrates to interpret the law more favourably to employers than had been planned. In November 1873 Gladstone's cabinet agreed to prepare a bill which would have been very similar to Disraeli's legislation (Matthew 1982: lxxvi–

lxxvii). Fittingly, the impetus for the peaceful picketing part of the legislation of 1875 came from Robert Lowe and other Liberals, after the Conservative leadership had dragged its feet. (Smith 1967: 216–17). Disraeli was euphoric about the new legislation, however: he told two of his female correspondents that 'We have settled the long and vexatious contest between capital and labour', and that, 'this is the greatest measure since the Short Time Act and will gain and retain for the Tories the lasting affection of the working classes' (ibid.: 216–17). This was extravagant language, but it was an accurate expression of the perceived novelty and success of this important initiative.

The spadework on the labour legislation had been performed by the home secretary, R. A. Cross, a surprise appointment whose populist Lancashire contacts and capacity for hard work helped to make him one of the great successes of the ministry. He was also the central figure in the preparation of the two measures of these years which went furthest in extending the role of the state in improving the living standards and working conditions of the working class. Cross was quick to respond, at the very beginning of the ministry, to the demand for a further reduction of the hours of labour in textile factories, and in 1875 he was the prime mover behind the Artizans Dwellings Act, which enabled urban local authorities to impose the compulsory purchase of unhealthy slums and oversee their replacement with planned housing. This activity was to be financed by government loans at low interest, but the houses themselves were, of course, to be built by private enterprise. This, said Disraeli, was 'our chief measure' and he had kept a benevolent eye on its gestation, although remaining for a long time vague about its actual content.

As with trade union reform, there was nothing specifically Tory about these acts. The Torrens Act of 1868, passed under the Liberals, would have covered similar ground to the Artizans Dwellings Act if its compulsory purchase clauses had not been blocked by the House of Lords, and the 1875 measure was heavily influenced by a committee of the Charity Organization Society which had members from both sides of the Commons, including Cross himself. The bill was supported by Liberals as well as Conservatives. This measure of consensus, which also applied to the factory hours legislation, is less surprising when the limited extent of the innovation is realized. The principle of factory hours limitation was well established, and Cross was careful to stress that he did not intend explicitly to protect the working conditions of men, who were supposed to be able to look after themselves, as well as of women and children. The housing legislation was so hedged around with restrictions, so expensive to implement, and so wedded to the principles of *laissez-faire*, that it was very little used and made little or no difference to the comfort of the actual slum-dwellers when it was. It was undoubtedly well-intentioned, and Disraeli clearly believed in it, but it was far from being a major new departure.

The other measures were less distinctive, and in some cases even less effective. The licensing law of 1874 was intended as a sop to the brewers, but in some areas it actually curtailed licensing hours still further, as eventually passed, and it ultimately satisfied nobody. The legislation on public health, river pollution and friendly societies enacted or codified the results of Royal Commissions which had been established under the previous ministry, and in the case of the friendly societies Cross revealed the extent of his *laissez-faire* assumptions by expressing doubts about whether the government should even be responsible for advising the societies about best practice and thereby helping to stabilize their finances. The river pollution measure failed either to define pollution or to provide ways of punishing polluters: here again, the interests of property and industry were sacrosanct. The merchant shipping measure also followed on from a Royal Commission, established in 1873, and what limited improvements it made to the safety of merchant seamen were due entirely to the agitation conducted by the Liberal MP for Derby, Samuel Plimsoll, and the worries of Conservative MPs for seaports who counted merchant seamen among their constituents. Here again, the government was unwilling to infringe the economic orthodoxy which left the negotiation of working conditions to the 'free' contract between employer and employee. The food adulteration legislation followed the report of a select committee, and its value was reduced by the failure to compel local authorities to appoint the analysts who were essential to the practical implementation of the law. This reflected the prevailing concern, which Disraeli shared very strongly, to protect the autonomy of local government against any dangerous expansion of the coercive powers of the state. Finally, the Education Act of 1876 increased the pressure on working-class parents to send their children to school, but its overriding aim was not so much to improve working-class education as to sustain the finances of the Church of England schools to which Conservatives were so deeply attached, and to avoid the spread of elective school boards into the countryside, where they would, said Lord Sandon,

> afford the platform and the notoriety specially needed by the political Dissenting Ministers (many of them, to my mind, the most active and effective revolutionary elements of the day), and also provide a ready machinery for lowering the legitimate and useful influence of the leading personages of the place.
>
> (quoted by Smith 1967: 249)

So this act, which did generate political controversy, was primarily about the preservation of the rural influence of the landed interest in rustic tranquillity, at a time when the recent emergence of agricultural trade unions was beginning to heighten fears about unrest among the lower orders.

This was, then, limited and piecemeal social reform: well described by Norton and Aughey as 'giving self-help an institutionalized push', and offering no opposition to established orthodoxies about the sanctity of property and the (very narrow) extent of the legitimate role of the state in the economy (Norton and Aughey 1981: 109). Disraeli presided over the passing of the legislation, without supplying a detailed agenda: his role was to make time available for a programme of this kind, and to supply a benign environment for it. Most of the actual legislation merely emerged: there was no need for an overall plan or set of priorities to identify problems and bring them into the parliamentary arena. And the only distinctively Conservative aspects of the legislation had nothing to do with its status as 'social reform': they were the parts of the Licensing and Education Acts which rewarded or protected Tory vested interests. The only *Disraelian* aspects were rhetorical.

Should we be surprised at this conclusion? Probably not. In the first place, we should not misunderstand the message of the 'Young England' novels. Disraeli looked to individuals – especially leaders and men of romantic genius – to lead the nation back into what he saw as its natural state of unity and freedom from conflict. He saw a role, however ill-defined, for the church, but above all he thought that social improvement and stability should come through the actions of aristocrats and employers who recognized that property entailed duties as well as rights. The state plays at best a very minor, supporting role in Disraeli's scheme, and in this respect Disraeli was very much a man of his time. The state and its legislative machinery might be used to right specific wrongs, and to restore the natural

53

harmony of interests between rich and poor when they were disrupted by such vices as greed, pride and ignorance, but it was not to be the main engine of amelioration. Thus Disraeli was generally friendly to factory legislation, without adopting a very high profile on the subject. Lord Shaftesbury in 1866 found him 'decided and true to the cause' in schemes for social improvement (Finlayson 1981: 470), but such schemes did not necessarily involve state intervention anyway, and in fact Disraeli's record was somewhat chequered. Most famously, he spoke and voted against the Mines Bill of 1850 (which would have provided for mines inspection) at the behest of the tyrannical coal-owner Lord Londonderry and his wife Frances Anne, whose salon Disraeli frequented. He also opposed legislation, like the Education Order of 1839 and the Public Health Act of 1848, which seemed to involve an unacceptable extension of the powers of central government. As Paul Smith makes clear, 'Disraeli's popular Toryism, in short, was an idea, an attitude, not a policy, and what its progenitor was calling for was a regeneration, not a reconstruction, of society' (Smith 1967: 17). This was as true of the 1870s as it was of the 1840s.

Moreover, although Disraeli might continue to pay lip service to the idea of 'One Nation', and in some significant sense to believe in it, the 1840s marked the high point of his interest in the lives of those who were outside the charmed aristocratic circles in which he mixed. His promotion of Cross and the bookstall magnate W. H. Smith to cabinet rank was a matter of political calculation rather than social principle, and in the late 1860s he discovered London's spreading suburbia with a sense of novelty and amazement: 'What miles of villas! and of all sorts of architecture! What beautiful churches! What gorgeous palaces of Geneva' (quoted by Blake 1969: 526). His general attitude to the middle classes exhibited an aristocratic suspicion and reserve: Derby remarked in 1877 on his 'odd dislike of middle-class men, though they are the strength of our party', and a little later commented, 'unfortunately the Premier neither likes nor understands the middle-class' (quoted by Swartz 1985: 52, 69). The Conservatives were beginning their transition to the guardianship of property of all kinds, not just landed property, but Disraeli was neither as responsive nor as enthusiastic towards this trend as has sometimes been suggested.

As for the working class, by the early 1870s Disraeli was capable of displaying a remarkable optimism about their circumstances. In 1871 he told the Commons:

The working classes are not paupers; on the contrary, they are a very wealthy class – they are the wealthiest in the country. Their aggregate income is certainly greater than any other class; their accumulations are to be counted by millions; and I am not speaking merely of the deposits in savings banks, but of funds of which I am aware they are in possession, and which are accumulated to meet their trade necessities and to defend their labour and rights.

> (*Hansard*, 3rd series, 208 (1871), 31 July, col. 589)

He was rightly taken to task about these half-truths and misleading statistics by the working-class journalist Thomas Wright (1873: 56), and this is a far cry from the relatively well-informed subdivision of the working class by occupation and culture which characterizes *Sybil*. If England was to be 'One Nation' in the 1870s, it was still to be so under the tutelage and in the chosen image of its aristocratic mentors, and this perception was increasingly predominant in the mind of Disraeli himself. It was unlikely that a well-informed programme of social reform, responding directly and empathetically to the needs of the working class, would emanate from such a source as this, and this was never Disraeli's goal anyway.

These attitudes are further expressed in Disraeli's attitude to the organization of the party at local level. He was unhappy about the emergence of working-class Conservative clubs in many of the boroughs after the Second Reform Act, and gave only 'lukewarm and reluctant' support to those of his younger colleagues who encouraged them. As Feuchtwanger points out, he 'did not approve of party organizations divided along class lines, when he was portraying the Tory party as a national party capable of uniting all classes' (1985: 48). Only when he appointed John Gorst, an activist in this movement, as central party organizer in 1870, and the working-men's clubs were brought under the control of constituency organization (and therefore of men of property and position), did he give full support to the spread of local popular Tory societies. Gorst and the new Conservative Central Office probably played a significant part in the 1874 election victory, although Disraeli, to Gorst's chagrin, subsequently lost interest and allowed the new system to wither on the vine. This was not as full or sustained a commitment to practical Tory democracy as the Disraeli legend might lead us to expect.

As P. R. Ghosh points out, the concept of 'social reform' as such was a novelty in the mid-1870s. It was regarded as a necessary but inferior kind of activity, complicated but unglamorous, and not a likely or proper arena for conflict between the parties. If pushed beyond consensus, it soon fell foul of a range of potent political taboos. It was likely to push rates and taxes up, at a time when there was considerable resistance in the Conservative Party, among farmers and others, to current levels. It could seem to take responsibilities away from individuals, where they were held to belong, and place them in the hands of the state, which would undermine independence and negate self-help. It would discriminate against the propertied and in favour of the propertyless. As Bruce Coleman reminds us, this is not what the Conservative Party was basically for. Its essential function was to protect and sustain the interests of substantial property-owners. (Coleman 1988: 3–4). It is therefore not surprising that even those reforms which were carried through in 1874–6 faced suspicion and sometimes outright opposition, within the cabinet as well as among the party's back-benchers. And the lack of sustained, vociferous working-class demand for most of the measures (trade union reform and merchant shipping apart) made life more difficult still for reformers. Feuchtwanger claims that, 'In 1875 the case of the Tichbourne claimant caused greater popular excitement than the social reform legislation. . . . An imposter laid claim to titles and attracted much sympathy among the lower classes (1985: 91). Under all the circumstances, it may well seem surprising that Conservative social reform found its way on to the agenda at all.

This perspective brings us to a fresh look at Disraeli. He may not have lived up to the expectations which are aroused by the Disraelian legend and the 'One Nation' myth, but here he may fall victim to his own presentational skills and those of subsequent propagandists. Looked at in the context of his time and ideas, he made a difference to the party's programme as well as to its image. His motives were hard-nosed as well as romantic. He feared for the future of the race, if the slums were to continue to breed teeming new generations with inferior bodies, minds and morals. He was acutely afraid of revolutionary societies and plots, and he was anxious to win the assent of the working class to the established economic and political order, without making concessions which might actually damage the position and resources of his propertied supporters. As he said in 1848, 'The palace is not safe when the cottage is not happy' (quoted by Blake 1969: 556). To this end, he sought to remove unnecessary grievances and to restore and sustain that state of harmony between rich and poor, employer and employee, which he held to be the natural state of society. The social reform programme of 1874–6 was a sustained gesture in that direction, and Disraeli promised it, publicized it, took ostentatious pride in it and allocated time to it, in a way that Gladstone never felt able to match. It is all very well, and salutary, to emphasize what Disraeli did not do, but what he *did* do was very important indeed, and it even made a difference, however small, to the living conditions of some of those at whom the legislation was directed.

P. R. Ghosh would go further than this, arguing that the Disraeli ministry of 1874–80 marked the real beginning of a lasting Conservative willingness to pursue policies of social amelioration through legislation. He points to a revival of social concerns in the session programme for 1880, despite what he admits to have been the 'legislative desert' of 1877–9, and he denies that Disraeli, in his last years, was irretrievably seduced by the pursuit of glory in international diplomacy. Above all, Disraeli played a major part in 'the seamless development of the Conservative reformist tradition from the institutional to the social sphere' (Ghosh 1987: 80). He helped to make social policy an accepted, uncontroversial (in principle) part of the Conservative agenda, and thereby extended the range of acceptable political concerns in a way that was ultimately socially stabilizing. Thus the developing Conservative tradition of social reform shored up and legitimized the constitution, and helped to reduce the scope for the emergence of a revolutionary politics.

In some respects, Ghosh probably goes too far. Most obviously, his discovery of a revived social programme in 1880 smacks of special pleading. There is little of substance to support his assertions. But it is helpful to be reminded of the arguments for Disraeli's importance. Most significant of all, however, is the persisting importance of the Disraelian legend, in this field as in others. At very least, this demonstrates formidable skills in self-presentation and the manufacture and management of myth. Here, Disraeli's romantic self-image, and his successful propagation of his sense of his own destiny and power into the outside world, is of central importance. He did not lose his charisma even in old age, despite his own awareness of failing energy during his only sustained period as prime minister. And it carried a powerful charge beyond the grave, to the lasting benefit of the Conservative Party in the twentieth century. As we evaluate Disraeli's overall performance on the political stage (an appropriate metaphor, no doubt), we shall also need to assess the nature of his legacy.

# 6
# Legend and legacy

How principled a politician was Disraeli? And what form, if any, did his principles take? Opinion is much less sharply polarized now than in his own time and in the decades immediately following his death, when some viewed him with veneration and others dismissed him as a schemer and charlatan who hid his opportunism behind a smokescreen of high-sounding phrases. Such views survived tenaciously within his own party, at least until the 1870s. Among Liberals they acquired added venom from the personal hatred which developed between Disraeli and Gladstone. Disraeli came to refer to Gladstone, habitually, as 'the A.V.' (the Arch-Villain), while in turn he once provoked Gladstone into saying 'Damn him!', a most uncharacteristic form of words, and Gladstone was unable to bring himself to attend Disraeli's funeral. These attitudes were carried to greater extremes among the rival supporters, especially when the dispute over the Eastern Question raged. As Blake suggests, 'These passions have been carried far beyond the grave . . . it is only fairly recently that people have at last been able to praise one of the great rivals without damning the other' (1969: 761).

Efforts to present Disraeli as a politician of principle are not helped by aspects of the way in which he presented himself. His self-conscious foreignness, the Byronic and Germanic romanticism through which he sought to kindle and display the peculiar genius which he saw within himself, his isolation from the main currents of English public school and university learning, and his idiosyncratic

59

ideas about religion and race, conspired to make him seem pretentious and self-seeking to prosaic parliamentary colleagues (Smith 1987). The hard shell of irony and the wounding repartee with which he shielded himself from a threatening world made him seem flippant and lacking in that *gravitas* which became increasingly important to the public face of a Victorian politician, even after he abandoned the exotic rings, gaudy finery and affectations of his early salon days. The impressions created by these raffish formative years were enduring: the whiffs of adulterous scandal from the 1830s were slow to disperse, and as Donald Southgate remarks, it was difficult for earnest churchmen 'to accept as a true believer a man who had muttered in drawing rooms, "Allah is great"' (Southgate 1977: 128). And at the very end of Disraeli's career his last novel, *Endymion*, left the Archbishop of Canterbury 'with a painful feeling that the writer considers all political life as mere play and gambling' (quoted by Blake 1969: 735). It was difficult to impute settled political principles to such a figure, especially after a generation of opposition had identified him as a master of the occult arts of forming unlikely alliances and nimbly changing direction on small matters in pursuit of short-term advantage. Some would have regarded the third Marquis of Salisbury, who was no friend to Disraeli, as being unduly generous when he remarked in the mid-1870s that his leader had no principle except that of maintaining party unity (Southgate 1977: 124), and any such principle had itself only come to the fore after Disraeli's own emergence as Conservative leader in the Commons.

We cannot usefully make retrospective judgements about Disraeli's sincerity. But we can go further than Salisbury did in identifying enduring principles which underlay Disraeli's political behaviour. Most obviously, his desire to preserve party unity was not an end in itself: it had a wider purpose. The Conservative Party was Disraeli's vehicle for restoring England to its 'natural' state of aristocratic rule, responsible government and social harmony. He sought to strengthen the traditional institutions of national and local government, combining a strong monarchy with a revitalized church, a powerful House of Lords and a healthy measure of independence for local government, from the generally squire-dominated Quarter Sessions of the counties to the borough, the manor and the parish. He saw the rule of the propertied, with due respect for the rights of the poor and due opportunity for the self-advancement of the ambitious, as the best guarantee of traditional liberties as well as of the rights of property. And he identified this vision of an organic society, one whose institutions had grown and adapted through the centuries, with fierce opposition to what he saw as the efforts of the Whigs to dismantle it and replace it by artificial institutions which were intended to perpetuate the rule of a narrow oligarchy in the interests of themselves rather than those of the nation as a whole. This was the root cause of the 'unnatural' social conflict of the Chartist years.

This version of how society ought to work could look authoritarian, and at times Disraeli was indeed suspected of wanting to revive royal powers, and even those of the House of Lords, at the expense of the Commons. And he was certainly no democrat in the sense of wishing to hand power over to the untrammelled voting preferences of a mass electorate. As Southgate, again, points out, this was entirely compatible with the eventual form taken by the Second Reform Act, which might seem an embarrassment to this presentation of Disraeli's political values. It was not a democratic measure: it aimed at representing the urban working class as an interest, or more accurately as an 'order' or 'estate of the realm': traditionalist terminology which reflects Disraeli's retrospective cast of mind. It was compatible with 'aristocratic government in the proper sense of the term – that is, a government by the best men of all classes', and with that 'spirit of the English constitution' which 'recognised not the rights of man or of numbers but orders and classes' (Southgate 1977: 162).

Not that Disraeli's ideas were set in concrete. The basis of his creed was set out in the political writings of the 1830s and the novels of the 1840s. The institutions and ideals he sought to defend and revive could not be artificially and anachronistically preserved unchanging in the turbulent world of the nineteenth century, however, and Disraeli was as much aware of that as Peel, although to describe the Conservative Party's practice under his leadership as 'Peelite', as Professor Gash and others have done, seems to beg a lot of questions (Ward 1974: 91–2). The most apposite rendering of Disraelian attitudes in this context may well be Lord Butler's:

Alas, feudalism and monasticism and lordship and kingship . . . and other features of the organic society cannot conceivably survive the impact of the almighty machine [of, presumably, economic and social change], but the *values* of that older society can and must somehow be made to survive, and that is what politics should be about.

(Butler 1977: 12)

61

The most obvious instance of Disraeli adapting his ideas to changing circumstances can be found in imperial policy. He can be acquitted of opportunistically changing course in his 1872 speeches: they were not inconsistent with his previous pronouncements in the ways that historians used to suggest. But he did give colonial and imperial themes a much higher profile in the latter stages of his career: though not as high as the Disraelian myth might lead us to believe. But Disraeli's version of imperialism was very much an overseas extension of 'One Nation', extending the benefits of the aristocratic constitution to distant races and cultures, while providing relief from potentially dangerous domestic conflicts, and a valuable source of national pride and unifying rhetoric. And his general foreign policy shows a striking degree of Palmerstonian continuity.

Some have suggested that Disraeli's political goals changed significantly after mid-century, when the disciplines of front-bench status pushed his earlier romantic prescriptions outside the pale of practical politics and imposed the constraints of 'the art of the possible'. Lewis goes further, arguing that the 'Young England' programme should be taken seriously as Disraeli's genuine prescription for the healing and revitalization of state and society, but that the revolutions and disturbances of 1848 brought about a lasting change in attitude. Henceforth, says Lewis, his dominant preoccupation was to keep revolution at bay, and his actions were the product of 'pure expediency' in pursuit of power for the furtherance of this overriding aim. Lewis emphasizes Disraeli's fear of European secret societies and revolutionary organizations, in which he did indeed take a morbid and romantic interest, and he points to the fears of the impending collapse of civilization which haunted Disraeli's last years. This is an interesting argument, but it underrates the positive side of Disraeli's political outlook, in the 1870s as in the 1840s, and evidence is too often distorted to fit the straitjacket of the interpretation, as when Disraeli's Londonderry-inspired opposition to the Mines Bill of 1850 is seen as part of a rapprochement with the middle classes rather than as a reaction to upper-class pressure from a patron.

More recently, Ghosh has argued that, 'It is possible to trace a continuous development in [Disraeli's] ideas from the late 1840s through to the end of his career' (1984: 286). At the core of this trend, for Ghosh, is the dictum that 'expenditure depends on policy'. Disraeli was a doctrinaire proponent of economy in government, and of low taxation: to have acted otherwise would have been electoral suicide in any case, given the expectations of the time. But he was not as rigid as Gladstone in keeping expenditure down whatever the circumstances: he 'did not seek economy for its own sake', and 'was happy to let expenditure expand freely within the limits imposed by the natural growth of the revenue' (Ghosh 1984: 287). This made room for higher spending on social policy and colonial wars, although it left both local government and the armed forces vulnerable to cutbacks in the hard times of the late 1870s. But this attitude to public spending was anathema to Gladstone and his followers, as P. W. Clayden showed in his anti-Disraeli polemic on the eve of the 1880 general election: 'Mr Gladstone would have made the policy of the Government fit in with his financial plans; Sir Stafford Northcote had to accommodate himself to the requirements of colleagues who were intent on everything but economy' (1880: 70). As Ghosh (1984) makes clear, this contemporary critique was grossly exaggerated, but its confident tone is indicative of the consensual nature of the financial orthodoxy with which Disraeli was faced.

These ideas form part of a wider reappraisal of Disraeli, in which Ghosh (1987) also provides controversial interpretations of foreign policy and social reform. However, they are not going unchallenged. Paul Smith comments that, 'Apart from making Disraeli sound dull', Ghosh's vision of Disraeli as 'a competitor with Gladstone for the Peelite mantle of economical finance and moderate progress' is profoundly misleading. It artificially divorces 'the professions of the 1830s and 1840s' from 'the mature political career', and it parades, as if they were of central importance, 'banal precepts [which] cannot do duty for the fundamentals of Disraeli's political outlook', which can be found in the earlier writings and were reiterated in the general preface to the new edition of Disraeli's novels which came out in 1870 (Smith 1987: 67–8). So Smith, who is dismissed by Ghosh as one of the 'neo-opportunist' school of Disraeli's interpreters, can now be found allying himself with those who lay stress on the enduring importance of principles which were enunciated at the outset of Disraeli's political career.

As was suggested by the discussion of financial policy, however, Disraeli's scope for actually moulding the pattern of events and setting the political agenda was severely constrained – both by consensus values, to most of which he himself subscribed anyway, and by external events such as the agricultural and trade depression of the late 1870s. Even when he came to power in 1874, with a resounding majority after all, his main commitment was to abstain from the sort of harassing and divisive legislation with which, he alleged, Gladstone had wearied the country. Social reform was a quiet, low-key alternative to such policies, and its positive attributes were given lower priority than the commitment to giving the nation a rest from controversial attacks on established institutions. There is much to be said for the view that Disraeli's contribution to the long-term fortunes of the Conservative Party has much more to do with ideas, slogans, rhetoric and presentation than with specific policies and actual legislation. Moreover, much of Disraeli's enduring image was generated by his opponents in the later stages of his career: from a legislation and foreign policy perspective he stands out in sharper relief as a result of Gladstonian propaganda than if his activities are evaluated dispassionately on their merits. A surprising number of the alleged differences between Gladstone and Disraeli were matters of presentation and histrionics: their policies and deeds were much less divergent than their speeches and their partisans made them appear.

Nor was the tenor of Disraeli's interpretation of social and political problems and their solution dramatically novel. Even the famous 'Two Nations' formula was not original, and Disraeli's invocation of feudal and paternalist virtues had plenty of contemporary echoes, and some contemporary inspiration, in the writings of Southey and Carlyle, Ruskin, and even Dickens. The first two of these were strong and direct influences on Disraeli, as, in a different idiom, was Byron. This is not to say that Disraeli was unoriginal: his polemical reconstruction of a Tory interpretation of English history since the Middle Ages was a particularly powerful and innovative contribution. But a lot of what he articulated was 'in the air' at the time anyway. His was indeed a distinctive voice, and his ideas were attractively presented. The novels can still be read with enjoyment, and continue to attract critical acclaim (Schwarz 1979). But part of Disraeli's strength was that he had plenty of intellectual company. He was no prophet crying in the wilderness, but very much in tune with important strands of contemporary thought.

In a sense, this makes the enduring power of the Disraelian legacy all the more striking, and it has had to be subtly remade, or at least reinterpreted, for popular consumption in each succeeding generation. At the most populist level, the Primrose League was founded in 1883 to realize the ideals of Tory democracy and 'One Nation' by the mobilization of a mass membership under the patronage of Tory dignitaries. Disraeli's supposed favourite flower supplied the name, and much was made each year of Primrose Day, 19 April, the anniversary of his death. At its peak in 1914 the league claimed 800,000 members, many in industrial areas, and it was particularly effective at attracting women to the Conservative cause (Pugh 1985): ch. 5). It continued to propagate a romantic view of Disraeli's life and works for many years, although by the early 1980s it had become 'more a congenial political and social gathering . . . than . . . a serious political force' (Norton and Aughey 1981: 234). Over the years, however, the Primrose League exposed a very large number of working-class converts to an essentially 'One Nation' version of what Conservatism was about.

The Disraelian legacy was given a new lease of life in the aftermath of the Second World War and the spectacular Labour victory in the 1945 General Election. Attempts to adapt the party to the post-war world featured the reiteration of Disraelian commitments to social reform. The One Nation Group emerged, seeking to 'reconcile an industrial democracy with economic and social inequalities'. As a contemporary wrote,

> The Conservative Party . . . has shown a willingness to drop its sterile laissez-faire philosophy in favour of a concept of government which, rooted in earlier Tory thinking and clearly expressed in the time of Disraeli, constitutes a constructive amalgamation of Conservatism and democracy.
>
> (Norton and Aughey 1981: 60)

It was not quite what Disraeli had meant by 'One Nation', but the words kept their incantatory power. The formula succeeded because:

> it did strike a chord in the minds of Conservatives. If it was a myth that Disraeli had something of practical significance to say to post-war Britain it was an effective myth. It established Conservative credentials to manage the new mixed economy and it represented the fashioning of an electorally successful image of Conservative compassion as well as competence.
>
> (ibid.: 78)

Meanwhile, R. J. White was providing a popular handbook of Tory beliefs, with a selection of key texts, and the introduction contained a hymn of praise to Disraeli and the organic view of how societies should work. With his 'wondrous imagination', Disraeli – unlike Peel – understood 'what society really is, and how it lives in its organic vitality':

He knew that there was a Tory tradition which answered to the nature of men in both their immediate and their ultimate purposes, the tradition of an organic as distinct from an artificial society, and he brought this great tradition into Conservatism as a constructive force for the furtherance of positive purposes.

(White 1950: 12–13)

So, far beyond the grave, Disraeli provided Conservatives with ideas, images and propaganda material, and his name remained a force to conjure with. His skills in presentation, which so often disguised a lack of firm legislative content, were bequeathed for the use of his successors in very different times.

In the Thatcher years, Disraeli's name ceased to be invoked by members of the cabinet. He has been pushed to the margins by the new right, whose supporters dominate the making and expression of Conservative policy. Mrs Thatcher's collected speeches contain no invocation of his name. And the Conservative philosopher, Roger Scruton, finds no room for an article on Disraeli in a collection of eighteen essays on 'Conservative thinkers' which contains pieces on Burke, Ruskin and Jane Austen, Hayek and Hegel. Nor are Disraeli's intellectual ancestors, Bolingbroke and Coleridge, among those present. A whole tradition has been laid aside. But it lives on among the so-called 'wets', and throughout the 1980s coded references to Disraeli and 'One Nation' have been used, at the party conference and elsewhere, to indicate dissent from the main lines of Thatcherite policy (Jenkins 1989: 96, 101, 177–8). Most recently, discussion of the European social charter has brought Disraeli's name into the arena again. Thus Edward Heath: 'Social policy is not socialism. It is a cheap slur or perhaps a muddled mind to try and connect the two. We Conservatives have possessed a social policy ever since Disraeli, more than a century ago' (quoted by the *Guardian*, 25 May 1989). A month later another prominent Tory dissident, Michael Heseltine, could be heard urging the government to 'admit the Churchillian, indeed Disraelian, legitimacy of the proposed . . . Social Charter' (quoted by the *Guardian*, 24 June 1989). So the Disraelian inheritance is alive and well, if currently excluded from influence on the highest levels of policy-making and image-forming, and there could be no better testimony to the enduring charisma of the ringing phrases which form his most potent legacy.

But Disraeli's influence did not stop at the Conservative Party. Alfred Orage, an eccentric but far from negligible socialist of the turn of the century, derived his 'neo-feudalism', which issued forth in the Guild Socialist movement, from Disraeli. This forms an interesting parallel to the influence of Ruskin's thought on the early leaders of the Labour Party, and constitutes a reminder of the broad sweep and undoctrinaire quality of some of Disraeli's ideas (Steele 1989). And Disraeli, along with Coleridge, helped to inform the ideas of the highly influential literary critic, F. R. Leavis, identifying and in some sense endorsing the idea of 'Old England' as an 'organic community', natural, evolving, whole and secure. Leavis was, indeed, characteristically kind about Disraeli's novels (ibid.; Williams 1963: 246–56).

Why has Disraeli endured? He embodies a romantic story: the outsider who makes good, the man of will who rises to the top by sheer determination as well as wit and charm. He spoke – and speaks – to an attachment to tradition and order, and to notions of *noblesse oblige*, which remain widespread (for whatever reasons) in English if not in British society. The seductive power of his oratory, too, has translated remarkably well on to the printed page, and it still has the capacity to tug the heart-strings even of the sceptical. R. J. White was well-advised, for example, to conjure up the following passage to introduce *The Conservative Tradition*:

> By the Conservative cause I mean the splendour of the Crown, the lustre of the Peerage, the privileges of the Commons, the rights of the poor. I mean that harmonious union, that magnificent concord of all interests, of all classes, on which our national greatness depends.
>
> (quoted by White 1950: 26)

But Disraeli's value to a party which still lacks a unified body of theory, and depends for its appeal on an uneasy mixture of 'common sense', self-interest, fear and tradition, goes deeper even than this. Not only does he offer an array of fine phrases to kindle and sustain enthusiasm and a sense of collective mission. He also has a special ingredient: a most unusual kind of charisma. Sir Ian Gilmour, writing from the left-wing of the party in 1977, put his finger on what it is, when he remarked, 'Disraeli was one of the few Tory leaders who has been able to bring warmth to Conservatism, and to add to its basic common sense a degree of romance, generosity and excitement' (Gilmour 1978: 86). This, above all, is what made, and makes, Disraeli different.

# Bibliography

Bellairs, C. E. (1977) *Conservative Social and Industrial Reform*, rev. edn, London.

Bentley, M. (1984) *Politics Without Democracy, 1815–1914*, London.

Blake, R. (1966) *The Conservative Party from Peel to Churchill*, London.

——(1969) *Disraeli*, London.

Blake, R. and Cecil, Hugh (eds) (1987) *Salisbury: The Man and His Policies*, London.

Brantlinger, P. (1977) *The Spirit of Reform*, Harvard.

Braun, Thom (1981) *Disraeli the Novelist*, London.

Briggs, A. (1987) *Victorian People* (2nd edn), London.

Butler, Lord (ed.) (1977) *The Conservatives: A History from their Origins to 1965*, London.

Chamberlain, M. (1983) *Lord Aberdeen*, London.

Clayden, P. W. (1880) *England under Lord Beaconsfield*, reprinted London 1971.

Cohn, B. S. (1984) 'Representing authority in Victorian India', in E. J. Hobsbawm and T. Ranger (eds), *The Invention of Tradition*, Cambridge.

Coleman, Bruce (1988) *Conservatism and the Conservative Party in Nineteenth-Century Britain*, London.

Conacher, J. B. (1972) *The Peelites and the Party System, 1846–52*, Newton Abbot.

Cowling, M. (1965) 'Disraeli, Derby and fusion, October 1865 to July 1866', *Historical Journal*, 8: 31–71.

68

Crosby, T. L. (1977) *English Farmers and the Politics of Protection*, Brighton.

Cunningham, H. (1971) 'Jingoism in 1877–78', *Victorian Studies*, 15: 428–53.

—— (1989) 'The language of patriotism', in R. Samuel (ed.), *Patriotism: The Making and Remaking of British National Identity*, I, London.

Davis, R. W. (1976) *Disraeli*, London.

Disraeli, B. (1835) *Vindication of the English Constitution*, London.

——(1881) *Novels and Tales*, 11 vols, London: Hughenden edn.

Durrans, P. J. (1981–2) 'A two-edged sword: the Liberal attack on Disraelian imperialism', *Journal of Imperial and Commonwealth History*, 10: 262–84.

Eldridge, C. C. (1973) *England's Mission*, London.

Feuchtwanger, E. J. (1968) *Disraeli, Democracy and the Tory Party*, Oxford.

—— (1985) *Democracy and Empire*, London.

Finlayson, G. B. A. M. (1981) *The Seventh Earl of Shaftesbury*, London.

Ghosh, P. R. (1984) 'Disraelian Conservatism: a financial approach', *English Historical Review*, 98: 268–96.

—— (1987) 'Style and substance in Disraelian social reform', in P. J. Waller (ed.), *Politics and Social Change in Modern Britain*, Brighton.

Gilmour, Sir Ian (1978) *Inside Right*, 1st edn, London.

Gladstone, W. E. (1971) *Midlothian Speeches, 1879*, ed. M. R. D. Foot, Leicester.

Harcourt, F. (1980) 'Disraeli's imperialism, 1866–1868: a question of timing', *Historical Journal*, 23: 87–109.

—— (1985–6) 'Gladstone, Monarchism and the "new" imperialism, 1868–74', *Journal of Imperial and Commonwealth History*, 14: 20–51.

Hardie, F. (1963) *The Political Influence of Queen Victoria 1861–1901*, 3rd edn, London.

Hobsbawm, E. J. and Ranger, T. (eds) (1984) *The Invention of Tradition*, Cambridge.

Hyam, R. and Martin, G. (1975) *Reappraisals in British Imperial History*, London.

Jenkins, P. (1989) *Mrs Thatcher's Revolution*, pbk edn, London.

Jerman, B. R. (1960) *The Young Disraeli*, Princeton.

Kerr, D. A. (1982) *Peel, Priests and Politics*, Oxford.

Koebner, R. and Schmidt, H. Dan (1964) *Imperialism: The Story and Significance of a Word*, Cambridge.

Levitas, R. (ed.) (1987) *The Ideology of the New Right*, Cambridge.

Lewis, C. J. (1960–1) 'Theory *versus* expediency in the policy of Disraeli', *Victorian Studies*, 4: 237–58.

Lloyd, T. (1968) *The General Election of 1880*, Oxford.

McDowell, R. B. (1959) *British Conservatism 1832–1914*, London.

Machin, G. I. T. (1977) *Politics and the Churches in Great Britain 1832–68*, Oxford.

—— (1987) *Politics and the Churches in Great Britain 1869–1921*, Oxford.

Matthew, H. C. G. (ed.) (1982) *The Gladstone Diaries*, 7, Oxford.

—— (1988) *Gladstone 1809–74*, Oxford.

Mendilow, J. (1986) *The Romantic Tradition in British Political Thought*, London.

Millman, R. (1979) *Britain and the Eastern Question 1875–1878*, Oxford.

Monypenny, W. F. and Buckle, G. E. (1910–20) *The Life of Benjamin Disraeli*, 6 vols, London.

Norton, P. and Aughey, A. (1981) *Conservatives and Conservatism*, London.

O'Gorman, F. (1986) *British Conservatism*, London.

O'Kell, R. (1986–7) 'Two nations, or one? Disraeli's allegorical romance', *Victorian Studies*, 30: 211–34.

Pinto-Duschinsky, M. (1967) *The Political Thought of Lord Salisbury 1854–68*, London.

Porter, B. (1975) *The Lion's Share*, London.

—— (1982) *Britain, Europe and the World 1850–1982: Delusions of Grandeur*, London.

Pugh, M. (1982) *The Making of Modern British Politics 1867–1939*, Oxford.

—— (1985) *The Tories and the People 1880–1935*, Oxford.

Read, D. (1987) *Peel and the Victorians*, Oxford.

Schwarz, D. R. (1979) *Disraeli's Fiction*, London.

Scruton, R. (ed.) (1988) *Conservative Thinkers*, London.

Seton-Watson, R. W. (1935) *Disraeli, Gladstone and the Eastern Question*, London.

Shannon, R. (1976) *The Crisis of Imperialism, 1865–1915*, pbk edn, London.

—— (1982) *Gladstone*, 1, *1809–65*, London.

Shaw, C. and Chase, M. (eds) (1989) *The Imagined Past: History and Nostalgia*, Manchester.

Smith, P. (1967) *Disraelian Conservatism and Social Reform*, London.

—— (1987) 'Disraeli's politics', *Transactions of the Royal Historical Society*, 37: 65–85.

Southgate, D. (1966) *The Most English Minister*, London.

—— (ed.) (1974) *The Conservative Leadership 1832–1932*, London.

—— (1977) 'From Disraeli to Law', in Lord Butler (ed.), *The Conservatives: A History from their Origins to 1965*, London.

Steele, T. (1989) 'From gentleman to superman: Alfred Orage and aristocratic socialism', in C. Shaw and M. Chase (eds), *The Imagined Past: History and Nostalgia*, Manchester.

Stembridge, S. R. (1965) 'Disraeli and the millstones', *Journal of British Studies*, 5: 122–39.

Stewart, R. (1971) *The Politics of Protection*, Cambridge.

—— (1978) *The Foundation of the Conservative Party, 1830–1867*, London.

Swartz, Helen M. and Swartz, Marvin (1975) *Disraeli's Reminiscences*, London.

Swartz, M. (1985) *The Politics of British Foreign Policy in the Era of Disraeli and Gladstone*, London.

Vincent, J. R. (ed.) (1978) *Disraeli, Derby and the Conservative Party*, Hassocks.

—— (1990) *Disraeli*, Oxford.

Ward, J. T. (1974) 'Derby and Disraeli', in D. Southgate (ed.), *The Conservative Leadership 1832–1932*, London.

White, R. J. (1950) *The Conservative Tradition*, London.

Williams, R. (1963) *Culture and Society 1780–1950*, 3rd edn, Harmondsworth.

Wright, Thomas (1873) *Our New Masters*, reprinted London, 1973.